TABLE OF CONTENTS

INTRODUCTION

WHAT ARE OPTIONS?

Financial markets are like giant playgrounds where people buy and sell different things. Imagine you're at a bazaar, and instead of just buying fruits or clothes, you can also buy and sell the rights to buy or sell stocks, which represent ownership in companies. These special rights are called options.

ROLE OF OPTIONS IN INVESTMENT STRATEGIES:

Now, let's talk about options. They are like magic tickets that give you special powers in the stock market. When you own an option, it's like having the right to decide if you want to buy or sell a stock at a certain price in the future. This can be super useful because it allows you to make smart moves, even if you don't have all the money right now.

Example: Imagine you want to buy a cool toy that costs $100, but you only have $80. You can't buy it now, right? Now, what if someone gives you a special coupon that lets you buy the toy for $80 anytime in the next month. That coupon is like an option. It gives you the choice to buy the toy at a fixed price later. If the toy's price goes up to $120, you can still get it for $80 using your special coupon. That's how options work in the stock market!

Options give investors these cool choices, making them like strategic tools for playing in the financial market playground. In this book, we'll explore how these magic tickets work, why they matter, and how you can use them to make smart moves in the exciting world of options trading. Ready to dive in? Let's go!

B. PURPOSE AND SCOPE OF THE BOOK

This book is like a friendly guide for anyone curious about making smart moves in the stock market. If you've ever wondered about those magical things called options and how they work, you're in the right place. Whether you're new to investing or have some experience, this book is here to help you understand options trading in a simple and fun way.

Example: Imagine you're in a big library, and you want to learn about a new game. This book is like the perfect game guide for beginners. It uses easy words and examples, so everyone can enjoy playing in the stock market game.

The main goal of this book is to make options trading easy to understand. We'll break down complex ideas into bite-sized pieces, so you can grasp the concepts without feeling overwhelmed. By the end of the book, you'll have the knowledge and confidence to step into the world of options trading.

C. BRIEF HISTORICAL CONTEXT OF OPTIONS TRADING

Let's take a quick journey through time to understand where options trading came from and how it evolved.

1. Origins of Options Trading:

Options trading isn't a new game; people have been using similar strategies for centuries. Back in ancient times, imagine you're a farmer, and you want to protect yourself from the uncertainty of crop prices. You could make a deal with another farmer to have the option to buy a set amount of your crops at a fixed price in the future. This way, you're both shielded from unexpected price changes, and that's essentially an early form of options trading.

Example: Picture two farmers in a village. Farmer A grows lots of apples, and Farmer B wants to make sure he can buy them at a known price. They agree that in three months, Farmer B can choose to buy apples from

Farmer A at a set price, no matter what the market price is. That's an ancient version of a call option!

<u>2.</u> Evolution in Financial Markets:

As societies developed, so did the way people traded options. Fast forward to more recent times, in the 20th century, when organized financial markets were taking shape. The Chicago Board Options Exchange (CBOE), created in 1973, was like the grand opening of a new marketplace. It standardized options trading, making it more like a friendly, organized game for everyone.

Example: Imagine you're in a bustling marketplace, and suddenly a new section opens up where people are trading options. The CBOE was like adding a special section where everyone could trade these unique contracts. It made options accessible to more people and brought a new level of order to the game.

So, the historical journey of options trading is like watching a game evolve from simple agreements between farmers to a sophisticated, organized activity in the heart of financial markets. In this book, we'll guide you through this evolution, helping you understand how options trading has become an integral part of the exciting world of finance. Ready for the adventure? Let's continue!

II. WHAT ARE OPTIONS?

A. DEFINITION AND BASIC CHARACTERISTICS

1. Contract between Two Parties:

Think of an option as a special agreement between two players in the stock market game. One player, let's call them the "option holder," gets a unique right. The other player, known as the "option seller," takes on a specific obligation. It's like making a deal where one person has a choice, and the other person has a commitment.

Example: Imagine you want to buy a rare comic book from your friend, but you're not sure if it'll become even more valuable. So, you make a deal with your friend. You give them a small amount of money, and in return, they promise to sell you the comic book at a fixed price anytime in the next month. That's a bit like an option contract!

2. Right to Buy or Sell an Underlying Asset:

Now, let's talk about the superpower that comes with an option - the right to buy or sell something cool, like a stock or a commodity. If you hold a "call" option, it's like having the power to buy that cool thing at a specific price. If you hold a "put" option, it's like having the power to sell that cool thing at a set price. But remember, having the right doesn't mean you have to use it. You can choose to use it or not, depending on what makes the most sense for you.

Example: Think of a call option as having a backstage pass to a concert. You have the right to buy a ticket at a fixed price, but you don't have to if you find a better deal. On the other hand, a put option is like having a return ticket for a concert you bought. You have the right to sell it at a fixed price, but if you decide to attend, you just keep the ticket as a souvenir.

Understanding options is like having secret keys to unlock exciting possibilities in the stock market. In the next chapters, we'll explore these keys, learn how to use them wisely, and discover the magic they bring to your investing journey. Ready for the adventure? Let's keep going!

B. TYPES OF OPTIONS

1. CALL OPTIONS

A call option is like holding a ticket to buy something (usually a stock) at a specific price in the future. It's like saying, "I believe the price of this cool thing is going up, and I want the option to buy it later at today's price." Call options are like bullish bets, giving investors the chance to benefit from a potential rise in the market.

Example: Let's say you believe a popular tech company's stock, currently at $100, will go up. You buy a call option with a strike price of $110 that expires in a month. If the stock price rises to $120, you can use your call option to buy it at the lower agreed-upon price of $110, making a profit.

2. PUT OPTIONS:

A put option is like having a ticket to sell something (again, usually a stock) at a specific price in the future. It's saying, "I think the price of this thing might go down, and I want the option to sell it later at today's price." Put options are like bearish bets, allowing investors to protect against potential declines in the market.

Example: Let's say you own a stock that's currently valued at $90, but you're worried it might drop. You buy a put option with a strike price of $85 that expires in two months. If the stock falls to $80, you can use your put option to sell it at the higher agreed-upon price of $85, preventing bigger losses.

Understanding call and put options is like having different tools in your financial toolbox. They give you the ability to play both sides of the market, whether you think it's going up or down.

C. KEY COMPONENTS OF AN OPTION CONTRACT

1. STRIKE PRICE:

The strike price is like the magical number that determines the buying or selling price of the underlying asset when the option is exercised. It's the pre-agreed amount set in the option contract, giving clarity to both the option buyer and seller.

Example: Imagine you have a call option for a popular smartphone company's stock with a strike price of $150. If the current stock price is $140, you have the right to buy shares at $150 when you exercise the option. Similarly, for a put option with a strike price of $120, you can sell the stock at $120 even if the market price drops.

2. EXPIRY DATE:

The expiry date is like the expiration date of a coupon. It's the specific date by which the option must be exercised or it becomes worthless. This time limit adds a sense of urgency and defines the period during which the option holder can make a move.

Example: Suppose you have a call option on a fashion company's stock with an expiry date in one month. If, by that date, the stock price hasn't reached the level you expected, you might choose not to exercise the option. The option then expires, and you move on.

3. OPTION PREMIUM:

The option premium is like the cost of getting the special rights associated with the option. It's the price the option buyer pays to the option seller for the privilege of having the choice to buy or sell the asset. This premium is inf uenced by various factors, including market conditions, volatility, and time remaining until expiration.

Example: Let's say you want to buy a call option for a gaming company's stock. The option seller quotes you a premium of $10. To acquire the right to buy the stock at the agreed-upon price, you pay the $10 premium. If the stock's price goes up, the option premium might increase too, allowing you to sell the option at a potential profit.

III. HOW OPTIONS WORK

Options are financial instruments that provide investors with unique opportunities to manage risk, speculate on market movements, and enhance portfolio returns. Understanding the mechanics of options is crucial for anyone venturing into the world of derivatives trading. In this we explore four basic options strategies.

1. LONG CALL:

You're feeling optimistic about a stock, so you buy a call option.

- If the stock price goes up, your potential profit is unlimited.

- If the stock price stays the same or goes down, your maximum loss is the premium you paid for the call.

Example: Imagine you buy a call option for a tech company's stock at a strike price of $120. If the stock price rises to $140, your potential profit is ($140 - $120) - Premium Paid. If the stock stays at $120 or drops, your loss is limited to the premium paid.

2. SHORT CALL:

You sell a call option, taking on an obligation.

- o Your maximum profit is the premium received.

- o Your maximum loss is unlimited if the stock price rises significantly.

Example: Suppose you sell a call option for a clothing brand's stock at a strike price of $50. If the stock price stays below $50, you keep the premium. However, if the stock soars to $70, your loss potential is unlimited.

3. LONG PUT:

You're cautious about a stock, so you buy a put option.

- o If the stock price goes down, your potential profit is unlimited.

- o If the stock price stays the same or goes up, your maximum loss is the premium you paid for the put.

Example: Imagine you buy a put option for a beverage company's stock with a strike price of $90. If the stock price drops to $80, your potential profit is ($90 - $80) - Premium Paid. If the stock stays at $90 or goes up, your loss is limited to the premium paid.

4. SHORT PUT:

You sell a put option, taking on an obligation.

- o Your maximum profit is the premium received.

- o Your maximum loss occurs if the stock price drops significantly.

Example: Suppose you sell a put option for a car manufacturer's stock at a strike price of $60. If the stock price stays above $60, you keep the premium. However, if the stock tumbles below $60, your loss potential is significant.

B. INTRINSIC VALUE AND TIME VALUE

1. UNDERSTANDING INTRINSIC VALUE:

Intrinsic value is like the real, tangible worth of an option. It represents how much the option is worth if it were exercised immediately. For call options, it's the difference between the stock's current market price and the call's strike price (if positive). For put options, it's the difference between the put's strike price and the stock's current market price (if positive).

Example: If you have a call option with a strike price of $100 and the stock is currently trading at $110, the intrinsic value is $10 ($110 - $100). This is because, if exercised now, you could make a $10 profit by buying the stock at $100 and selling it at the market price of $110.

2. IMPACT OF TIME ON OPTIONS:

Time is like a ticking clock for options. As each day passes, the option's value can change. This change is known as time decay. The closer an option gets to its expiration date, the faster its time value erodes. Time value is the part of the option's premium that reflects the possibility of the stock moving in a favorable direction before expirction.

Example: Consider a call option on a tech stock with a strike price of $120. If the stock is currently at $115, the call option might still have value because there's time for the stock to rise. As the expiration date approaches, the time value decreases. If the stock doesn't rise, the option's value may decline, emphasizing the importance of time awareness in options trading.

Understanding intrinsic value and time value is like having two lenses to look at an option's worth. The intrinsic value represents the concrete profit potential based on current market conditions, while time value considers the potential for market movement before the option expires.

IV. OPTION PRICING

A. FACTORS INFLUENCING OPTION PRICES

1. UNDERLYING STOCK PRICE:

Influence: The current price of the underlying stock has a direct impact on option prices. For call options, as the stock price rises, the potential for profit increases, leading to higher call option prices. Conversely, for put options, as the stock price falls, the potential for profit grows, resulting in higher put option prices.

Example: If a tech company's stock is currently trading at $150, a call option with a strike price of $140 may have a higher premium than the same option with a strike price of $160 because the potential profit is more significant with the lower strike price.

2. TIME TO EXPIRATION:

Time is a crucial factor in option pricing. The longer the time remaining until the option expires, the higher the option premium, especially if the option is in the money or has the potential to move into the money.

Example: Consider two call options on a fashion company's stock with the same strike price. One option expires in one month, and the other expires in six months. The six-month option may have a higher premium because it provides the holder with a more extended period for the stock to potentially move favorably.

3.IMPLIED VOLATILITY:

Influence: Implied volatility reflects the market's expectation of future price fluctuations. Higher volatility typically leads to higher option premiums because there is a greater likelihood of significant price movements, increasing the potential for profit.

Example: In a volatile market where a tech company's stock is experiencing rapid price changes, call and put options on that stock may have higher premiums compared to a stable market environment.

4. INTEREST RATES

Interest rates also play a role in option pricing. Higher interest rates generally result in higher call option premiums and lower put option premiums. This is because the opportunity cost of tying up money in an option is higher when interest rates are elevated.

Example: If interest rates are on the rise, an investor might expect higher premiums for call options, making it more expensive to purchase the right to buy a stock at a fixed price.

B. INTRODUCTION TO THE BLACK-SCHOLES MODEL

The Black-Scholes Model is like a wizard's spellbook in the world of options trading. It's a mathematical formula that helps estimate the theoretical price of European-style options (options that can only be exercised at expiration). Developed by economists Fisher Black, Myron Scholes, and Robert Merton in the early 1970s, this model considers factors like the current stock price, time until expiration, the option's strike price, implied volatility, and interest rates.

Example: Imagine you have a call option on a tech company's stock, and you want to know its theoretical price using the Black-Scholes Model. You'd plug in the current stock price, the option's strike price, time until expiration, implied volatility, and interest rates into the formula to get an estimate. This model is like a magical tool that helps traders understand the fair value of options.

C. UNDERSTANDING GREEKS: DELTA, GAMMA, THETA, VEGA

1. DELTA:

Delta is like a superhero cape for options traders. It represents the sensitivity of an option's price to changes in the underlying stock price. For call options, delta is positive, indicating how much the option price might change for a $1 increase in the stock price. For put options, delta is negative, showing how much the option price might change for a $1 decrease in the stock price.

Example: If you have a call option with a delta of 0.7, it suggests that for every $1 increase in the stock price, the option price might increase by $0.70.

2. GAMMA:

Gamma is like the sidekick to delta. It measures the rate at which delta changes concerning changes in the underlying stock price. Gamma is essential for understanding how delta might change as the stock price moves.

Example: If you have c call option with a gamma of 0.05, it suggests that the delta might increase by 0.05 for a $1 increase in the stock price.

3. THETA:

Theta is like the ticking clock of options. It represents the sensitivity of an option's price to the passage of time. As each day passes, theta measures how much the option price might cecrease.

Example: If you have an option with a theta of -0.03, it suggests that the option price might decrease by $0.03 each day, all else being equal.

4. VEGA:

Vega is like the weather vane for implied volatility. It measures how much an cption's price might change for a 1% change in implied volatility.

Example: If you have an option with a vega of 0.02, it suggests that the option price might increase by $0.02 for every 1% increase in implied volatility.

V. RISKS AND REWARDS IN OPTIONS TRADING

A. RISK MANAGEMENT

1. LIMITED RISK OF BUYING OPTIONS:

Buying options is like paying for insurance. You invest a smaller amount (the premium) with the potential for significant returns, but you're aware that the maximum loss is limited to the premium paid. This limited risk is a key advantage for option buyers, providing a predetermined and manageable level of exposure.

Example: If you buy a call option for $200, your maximum risk is limited to the $200 premium you paid. Even if the option doesn't perform as expected and becomes worthless, your loss is confined to the initial investment.

2. UNLIMITED RISK OF SELLING OPTIONS:

Selling options, also known as writing options, involves taking on an obligation. While it generates immediate income (the premium received), the risk is potentially unlimited. For example, selling a call option exposes you to unlimited losses if the underlying stock's price rises significantly.

Example: Suppose you sell a put option for a premium of $150, granting someone the right to sell you a stock at a certain price. If the stock's price plummets, your potential loss is not capped at the $150 premium received. Instead, it could be substantial.

B. REWARDS AND OPPORTUNITIES

1. LEVERAGE AND POTENTIAL RETURNS:

Leverage in options trading is like using a magnifying glass on your investment. With a relatively small amount of money, you can control a more substantial position in the market. This amplification of your trading power can lead to higher potential returns. However, it's essential to recognize that leverage works both ways – while it can boost profits, it also magnifies losses.

Example: If you buy a call option for $500 to control 100 shares of a stock, and the stock price increases, the percentage gain on your initial investment can be much higher than if you had bought the stock outright. However, if the stock price doesn't move as expected, your loss is limited to the $500 premium paid.

2. DIVERSIFICATION STRATEGIES:

Options trading offers creative ways to diversify your investment portfolio. By incorporating different options strategies, you can potentially profit from various market conditions – whether it's bullish, bearish, or neutral. This flexibility allows you to adapt your portfolio to changing market dynamics and reduce risk by not relying solely on one investment strategy.

Example: Suppose you own a portfolio of technology stocks, and you're concerned about a potential market downturn. You could use options to implement a protective strategy, such as buying put options or employing a collar strategy, to hedge against potential losses in your stock holdings.

Understanding the rewards and opportunities in options trading is like discovering hidden treasures in the financial markets. In the upcoming chapters, we'll delve into specific options trading strategies, providing you with the tools to unlock these opportunities while managing risks effectively. Ready for the adventure? Let's continue the journey!

VII. OPTIONS TRADING TERMINOLOGY

A. BASIC TERMINOLOGY

IN-THE-MONEY (ITM):

An option is in-the-money (ITM) when its intrinsic value is positive. For a call option, this means the underlying stock's current market price is higher than the call's strike price. For a put option, it means the stock's market price is lower than the put's strike price.

- o **Example:** If you have a call option with a strike price of $50 and the stock is currently trading at $55, the call option is in-the-money.

AT-THE-MONEY (ATM):

An option is at-the-money (ATM) when its strike price is approximately equal to the current market price of the underlying stock.

- o **Example:** If a stock is trading at $100, a call option with a strike price of $100 and a put option with a strike price of $100 are considered at-the-money.

OUT-OF-THE-MONEY (OTM):

Concept: An option is out-of-the-money (OTM) when its intrinsic value is zero. For a call option, this occurs when the underlying stock's current market price is lower than the call's strike price. For a put option, it happens when the stock's market price is higher than the put's strike price.

- o **Example:** If you have a call option with a strike price of $60 and the stock is trading at $55, the cal option is out-of-the-money.

LONG POSITION:

Taking a long position in an option means buying the option with the expectation that its value will increase. It can refer to buying a call option if you anticipate the stock's price will rise or buying a put option if you expect the stock's price to fall.

- o **Example:** If you buy a call option for a tech company's stock, you have taken a long position, expecting the stock price to increase.

SHORT POSITION:

Taking a short position in an option involves selling the option with the hope that its value will decrease. It can refer to selling a call option if you believe the stock's price won't rise significantly or selling a put option if you think the stock's price won't fall substantially.

- o **Example:** If you sell a put option for a clothing brand's stock, you have taken a short position, expecting the stock price to remain above the put's strike price.

B. UNDERSTANDING OPTION SYMBOLS AND OPTION CHAINS

1. DECODING OPTION SYMBOLS:

Option Symbol Components:

Root Symbol: The root symbol represents the underlying asset or stock. It is usually one to five letters and helps identify the stock associated with the option. *Example:* For Apple Inc., the root symbol might be "AAPL."

Expiration Code: A single-letter code representing the expiration month for the option. For instance, "A" might represent January, "B" for February, and so on. *Example:* If you see "AAPL Jan 23," it indicates an option expiring in January 2023.

Strike Price Code: A numeric code representing the option's strike price. This code is often followed by additional letters to differentiate multiple options with the same strike price. *Example:* If the strike price is $150, the code might be "150."

Call/Put Code: A single-letter code indicating whether the option is a call (C) or put (P). *Example:* If it's a call option, you'll see "C," and if it's a put option, you'll see "P."

<u>Putting it All Together:</u>

Example Option Symbol: AAPL Jan 23 150 C

Root Symbol: AAPL (Apple Inc.)

Expiration Code: Jan 23 (January 2023)

Strike Price Code: 150 (Strike price of $150)

Call/Put Code: C (Call option)

READING AND INTERPRETING OPTION CHAIN DATA:

OPTION CHAIN COMPONENTS:

STRIKE PRICES:

The various prices at which options are available for a particular expiration date. These are arranged from lowest to highest. *Example:* A list of strike prices for AAPL options expiring in January 2023 might include $140, $145, $150, and so on.

CALL AND PUT COLUMNS:

The option chain displays call options on one side and put options on the other. Each column provides information about the respective options, including the last traded price, bid-ask spread, and volume. *Example:*

For a call option, you might see columns like Last, Bid, Ask, and Volume.

OPEN INTEREST:

The total number of outstanding contracts for a particular option. It represents the number of contracts that have not been closed or exercised. *Example:* If the open interest for a call option is 500, it means there are 500 contracts still active.

Implied Volatility (IV): A measure of the market's expectations for future price volatility. Higher implied volatility often leads to higher option premiums. *Example:* An implied volatility of 30% suggests that the market anticipates a 30% annualized price movement for the underlying stock.

Interpreting Option Chain Data:

a) Higher bid-ask spreads may indicate lower liquidity.
b) High open interest can suggest increased market interest in a particular option.
c) Volume indicates the number of contracts traded during a specific time period.

X. TIPS FOR SUCCESS

1. **Rules Are Your Ruler**: The strategy, your pre-defined risk limits, and trading plan provide structure. When violated, step back and reassess.

2. **Patience Pays**: Wait for candle closes at critical levels, never force trades, and use "no trade" days strategically for observation and learning.

3. **Risk Before Reward**: Position sizing reflects setup strength (stronger = possibly larger, weaker = smaller). Know your non-negotiable stop-loss BEFORE placing an order.

4. **Structure is Supreme**: Analyze the bigger picture using multiple timeframes. Does the overall market context support your planned short or long trade? Fight against, not with, the dominant flow.

5. **Strategies Purity**: Master the core concepts of trend, CPR, and support/resistance before adding unnecessary complexity. Too many indicators slow your decisions.

6. **Partial Profit Protection**: Book some gains near previous swing highs/lows – these act as

temporary barriers. Take money off the table while staying active.

7. **Adaptive Risk Management**: Learn the art of trailing stops for some flexibility but avoid being shaken out by normal volatility. Wide, fixed stops limit your potential.

8. **Winners Need Space (Sometimes)**: If a trade breaks significant levels with momentum and maintains strong Strategies signals, it may be profitable to ride a portion longer, protecting profits on the rest.

9. **News = Volatility**: High-impact events derail setups. Consider profit preservation BEFORE surprises happen, or adjust position sizing if you anticipate wild swings.

10. **The Critical Filter**: Impulsive moves often stem from impatience and greed. Ask: Does this trade TRULY meet my core Strategies criteria, or am I succumbing to emotion?

11. **Lessons in Losses**: Analyze losing trades objectively. Are there recurring weaknesses in your strategy or emotional blindspots? Great traders evolve after mistakes.

12. **Don't Feed the Greed Monster**: Use targets, partial profit-taking, and discipline to combat

unrealistic goals. Giving back profits is demoralizing and counterproductive.

13. **Stay Alert on Mondays**: Weekend excitement can create over-eagerness at the week's open. Be especially mindful of impulsive trading during this time.

14. **Honest Foundation**: Success requires brutal self-assessment. Identify weaknesses, seek improvement, and ditch your ego at the door.

15. **Your Instruments, Your Strengths**: Focus on understanding a handful of markets or assets in depth for the best edge.

16. **Adapt or Get Left Behind**: Market conditions change; can your strategy and mindset adjust, or is it best to sit out until conditions suit it?

17. **Buffer for Unknowns**: Unexpected life events happen. Ensure you have some cash cushion outside your actively traded capital to protect your trading journey.

18. **Scaling Up Too Fast**-Early wins tempt larger trades without earned confidence. One bad outcome destroys gains and confidence. Start small, scale-up systematically based on proven performance.

19. **Continuous Improvement**-Markets, your skills – always evolve. Analyze past trading, seek new concepts, test Strategies optimizations on historical data to stay ahead

20. **Don't Try to Outsmart the Market**-Forcing low-odds setups, expecting your genius overtakes the market – you'll lose. Stick religiously to your clear Strategies criteria; no setup, no trade.

OPTION SELLING

A short straddle, also known as a sell straddle, is an options trading strategy where an investor simultaneously sells a call option and a put option with the same strike price and expiration date. This strategy profits from low volatility, as the goal is for the underlying asset's price to remain relatively stable and close to the chosen strike price at expiration.

In the dynamic landscape of financial markets, traders are often drawn to the allure of speculative gains through options trading. However, amidst the excitement of buying options, there lies a lesser-known yet potentially more lucrative strategy: option selling. In this chapter, we'll explore the art and science of option selling, backed by practical examples, to help you harness its power effectively.

The Allure of Option Selling

Imagine you own a portfolio of blue-chip stocks, and you're looking to enhance your returns while managing risk. Option selling presents an enticing opportunity. Let's consider a hypothetical scenario:

You own 100 shares of XYZ Corp., currently trading at $50 per share. Instead of merely holding onto your stock, you decide to sell covered call options against your shares. You sell one call option with a strike price of \$55 and an expiration date one month away, for which you receive a premium of \$2 per share (\$200 in total).

Scenario 1: Stock Price Remains Below the Strike Price

At expiration, XYZ Corp. is trading below \$55 per share. The call option expires worthless, and you retain ownership of your shares. You've successfully pocketed the \$200 premium as income, effectively boosting your returns from holding the stock.

Scenario 2: Stock Price Rises Above the Strike Price

If XYZ Corp. surges above \$55 per share at expiration, the call option may be exercised by the buyer. You're obligated to sell your shares at the agreed-upon strike price of \$55, regardless of the current market price. While you miss out on potential gains above \$55, you still retain the premium received, cushioning the impact of selling at a lower-than-market price.

Strategies for Success

Option selling offers various strategies tailored to different market conditions. Let's explore another example:

Consider a scenario where you're bullish on a particular stock, but you're unwilling to commit significant capital to purchase it outright. Instead, you decide to sell cash-secured put options. Let's say you sell one put option with a strike price of $45 and an expiration date one month away, receiving a premium of $3 per share ($300 total).

Scenario 1: Stock Price Remains Above the Strike Price

At expiration, the stock is trading above $45 per share. The put option expires worthless, and you retain the entire premium received as income. You've effectively earned a return on capital without ever owning the underlying stock.

Scenario 2: Stock Price Falls Below the Strike Price

If the stock price declines below $45 per share at expiration, the put option may be exercised by the buyer. You're obligated to purchase the shares at the agreed-upon strike price of $45, regardless of the current market price. While this entails acquiring the stock at a potentially lower price, you still retain the premium received, reducing your effective purchase price.

Option Selling on Index: Intraday Straddles

In addition to individual stocks, option selling strategies can be applied to index options, offering opportunities for intraday trading. Let's consider an example:

You're analyzing the S&P 500 index, which is currently trading at 4000. Anticipating heightened volatility ahead of an important economic announcement, you decide to execute an intraday straddle strategy. You simultaneously sell both a call option and a put option with a strike price of 4000 and the same expiration date.

Scenario 1: Limited Market Movement

If the market remains relatively stable, the call and put options may expire worthless, allowing you to retain the entire premium received from selling both options.

Scenario 2: Significant Market Volatility

In the event of substantial market volatility, either the call or put option may be exercised, resulting in potential losses. However, the premium received from selling both options helps offset any losses incurred, providing a degree of protection.

Risk Management Techniques

Despite the benefits of option selling, prudent risk management is essential. Let's discuss an example:

Suppose you've been consistently selling covered calls against your stock holdings to generate income.

However, you recognize the risk of potential losses if the stock experiences a sharp rally beyond the strike price of your calls. To mitigate this risk, you decide to implement a stop-loss order, automatically closing out your covered call positions if the stock price surpasses a certain threshold, thereby limiting potential losses.

Conclusion: Embracing the Potential of Option Selling

Option selling offers a versatile and potentially lucrative approach to navigating financial markets. By understanding its advantages, employing strategic selling strategies, and implementing robust risk management techniques, traders can unlock a wealth of opportunities to enhance returns and manage risk effectively.

In the following chapters we will discuss some of the commonly used option selling strategies commonly used by traders

SHORT STRADDLE

A short straddle, also known as a sell straddle, is an options trading strategy where an investor simultaneously sells a call option and a put option with the same strike price and expiration date. This strategy profits from low volatility, as the goal is for the underlying asset's price to remain relatively stable and close to the chosen strike price at expiration.

EXAMPLE:

Suppose a stock is trading at $150. An investor executes a short straddle by selling both a call option and a put option with a strike price of $150 and the same expiration date.

KEY COMPONENTS:

1. **Options Sold:**

a) **Sell Call Option:** The investor sells a call option with a strike price of $150.
b) **Sell Put Option:** The investor sells a put option with a strike price of $150.

2. **Same Expiration Date:**

- Both the call and put options have the same expiration date.

STRATEGY GOALS:

1. **Profit from Low Volatility:**

- The short straddle profits when the underlying asset's price remains close to the chosen strike price at expiration.

2. **Premium Collection:**

- The investor aims to collect premiums from both the call and put options, generating income.

RISKS AND CONSIDERATIONS:

1. **Limited Profit Potential:**

The maximum profit is achieved if the underlying asset's price closes exactly at the chosen strike price at expiration. Profits decrease as the price deviates from the strike.

2. **Unlimited Loss Potential:**

Losses can be unlimited if the underlying asset's price makes a significant move away from the chosen strike in either direction.

3. **Impact of Volatility:**

High volatility can increase the risk of substantial price movements, impacting the strategy negatively.

4. **Time Decay Impact:**

Time decay is beneficial for the short straddle. The strategy profits from the erosion of the call and put options' time value.

EXAMPLE SCENARIO:

Suppose a stock is trading at $150. An investor executes a short straddle by selling both a call and put option with a strike price of $150. The premiums collected for each option are as follows:

- **Sell Call Option Premium: $5**

- **Sell Put Option Premium: $4**

- **Net Premium Received: $9**

OUTCOMES AT EXPIRATION:

1. **If the Stock Closes at $150:**

The short straddle achieves its maximum profit, which is the net premium received.

2. **If the Stock Deviates from $150:**

Profit decreases as the stock deviates from the $150 strike. Losses start accumulating if the stock makes a significant move in either direction.

4. **WHEN TO USE:**

Expectation of Low Volatility: The short straddle is suitable when an investor expects low volatility, and the underlying asset is anticipated to remain close to a specific price.

Income Generation: This strategy is employed to generate income through the premiums collected from selling both call and put options.

STRATEGY ADJUSTMENT:

Rolling the Position: If the stock price starts moving significantly in one direction, an investor might consider rolling the position by buying back the current options and selling new ones with different strike prices or expiration dates.

The short straddle is a strategy that thrives in low-volatility environments, providing a limited-profit, unlimited-risk position. Traders employing this strategy aim for the underlying asset to stay close to a specific price at expiration, maximizing premium collection. Thorough analysis of market conditions and potential price movements is essential for successful implementation.

SHORT STRANGLE

A short strangle is an options trading strategy where an investor simultaneously sells an out-of-the-money (OTM) call option and an OTM put option with different strike prices but the same expiration date. This strategy profits from low volatility, as it benefits when the underlying asset's price remains within a certain range.

EXAMPLE:

Suppose a stock is trading at $150. An investor executes a short strangle by selling a call option with a strike price of $160 and a put option with a strike price of $140, both with the same expiration date.

KEY COMPONENTS:

OPTIONS SOLD:

a) **Sell Call Option (OTM):** The investor sells a call option with a strike price higher than the current market price (out-of-the-money).

b) **Sell Put Option (OTM):** The investor sells a put option with a strike price lower than the current market price (out-of-the-money).

SAME EXPIRATION DATE:

Both the call and put options have the same expiration date.

STRATEGY GOALS:

1. Profit from Low Volatility:

The short strangle profits when the underlying asset's price remains within a certain range, allowing both the call and put options to expire worthless.

2. Premium Collection:

The investor aims to collect premiums from both the call and put options, generating income.

RISKS AND CONSIDERATIONS:

1. Limited Profit Potential:

The maximum profit is achieved if the underlying asset's price remains between the strike prices of the call and put options at expiration.

2. Unlimited Loss Potential:

Losses can be unlimited if the underlying asset's price makes a significant move beyond the strike prices in either direction.

3. Impact of Volatility:

High volatility can increase the risk of substantial price movements, impacting the strategy negatively.

4. **Time Decay Impact:**

Time decay is beneficial for the short strangle. The strategy profits from the erosion of the call and put options' time value.

EXAMPLE SCENARIO:

Suppose a stock is trading at $150. An investor executes a short strangle by selling a call option with a strike price of $160 and a put option with a strike price of $140. The premiums collected for each option are as follows:

- **Sell Call Option Premium: $3**

- **Sell Put Option Premium: $4**

- **Net Premium Received: $7**

5. OUTCOMES AT EXPIRATION:

1. **If the Stock Closes Between $140 and $160:**

The short strangle achieves its maximum profit, which is the net premium received.

2. **If the Stock Deviates Outside the Range:**

Profit decreases as the stock deviates from the $140 and $160 strike prices. Losses start accumulating if the stock makes a significant move beyond the strike prices.

WHEN TO USE:

Expectation of Low to Moderate Volatility: The short strangle is suitab e when an investor expects low to moderate volatility. and the underlying asset is anticipated to remain within a specific price range.

Income Generation: This strategy is employed to generate income through the premiums collected from selling both call and put options.

STRATEGY ADJUSTMENT:

Rolling the Position: If the stock price starts moving significantly in one direction, an investor might consider rolling the position by buying back the current options and selling new ones with different strike prices or expiration dates.

The short strangle is a strategy that thrives in a neutral to mildly volatile market, providing a limited-profit, unlimited-risk position. Traders employing this strategy aim for the underlying asset to stay within a certain range at expiration, maximizing premium collection.

LONG CALL BUTTERFLY

A long call butterfly, also known as a call spread butterfly, is an options trading strategy that involves combining three different call options to create a position that benefits from low volatility and minimal price movement in the underlying asset. This strategy is executed using three strike prices with the same expiration date.

Example: Suppose a stock is trading at $100. An investor executes a long call butterfly by simultaneously buying one lower strike call option (in-the-money), selling two middle strike call options (at-the-money), and buying one higher strike call option (out-of-the-money).

KEY COMPONENTS:

1. Call Options:

A long call butterfly involves three call options with the same expiration date.

a) **Lower Strike Call (ITM):**

The investor buys one call option with a lower strike price, which is in-the-money (ITM).

b) **Middle Strike Calls (ATM):**

The investor sells two call options with middle strike prices, which are at-the-money (ATM).

c) **Higher Strike Call (OTM):**

The investor buys one call option with a higher strike price, which is out-of-the-money (OTM).

2. Same Expiration Date:

All three call options in the long call butterfly have the same expiration date.

C. STRATEGY GOALS

1. Low Volatility Profit:

The long call butterfly profits from low volatility. The goal is for the underlying asset to remain close to the middle strike price at expiration.

2. Limited Risk and Reward:

The strategy has a limited risk and limited reward profile. The maximum loss occurs if the stock price makes a significant move away from the middle strike prices, and the maximum gain occurs if the stock price closes at the middle strike at expiration.

D. RISKS AND CONSIDERATIONS:

1. Limited Profit Potential:

The maximum profit potential is achieved if the stock price closes exactly at the middle strike price at expiration. Profits decrease as the stock price deviates from the middle strike.

2. Limited Loss Potential:

The maximum loss is limited to the net premium paid to establish the butterfly spread. This occurs if the stock price moves significantly away from the middle strike in either direction.

3. Time Decay Impact:

Time decay can impact the profitability of the long call butterfly. The strategy benefits from the passage of time if the stock price remains near the middle strike.

E. EXAMPLE SCENARIO:

Suppose a stock is trading at $120. An investor executes a long call butterfly with the following call options:

- **Lower Strike Call (ITM):**

Buy one call option with a strike price of $110 for a premium of $5.

- **Middle Strike Calls (ATM):**

Sell two call options with a strike price of $120 for a premium of $3 each.

- **Higher Strike Call (OTM):**

Buy one call option with a strike price of $130 for a premium of $2.

- **Net Premium Paid:**

The net premium paid is $2 ([$5 + $2] - [$3 + $3]).

- **Outcomes at Expiration:**

a) If the stock closes at $120, the middle strike, the long call butterfly achieves its maximum profit.

b) If the stock deviates from $120, the profit decreases, reaching a maximum loss if the stock makes a significant move away from the middle strike.

F. WHEN TO USE

- **Expectation of Low Volatility:**

The long call butterfly is effective when an investor expects low volatility, and the underlying asset is anticipated to remain close to a specific price.

- **Neutral Outlook:**

This strategy is suitable when the investor has a neutral outlook and doesn't anticipate significant price movements in the underlying asset.

G. STRATEGY ADJUSTMENT:

Adjusting Strike Prices:

If the stock price starts moving significantly in one direction, an investor might consider adjusting the strike prices to adapt to the changing market conditions.

The long call butterfly is a strategy that thrives in low-volatility environments, providing a limited-risk, limited-reward position. Traders employing this strategy aim for the underlying asset to stay close to a specific price at expiration. Thorough analysis of market conditions and potential price movements is essential for successful implementation.

LONG CALL CALENDAR SPREAD

A. DEFINITION

A long call calendar spread, also known as a time spread or horizontal spread, is an options trading strategy that involves buying c longer-term call option and selling a shorter-term call option with the same strike price. Both options have the same underlying asset and are typically executed simultaneously.

Example: Suppose a stock is trading at $100. An investor executes a long call calendar spread by buying a call option expiring in three months with a strike price of $105 and simultaneously selling a call option expiring in one month with the same $105 strike price.

B. KEY COMPONENTS

1. Call Options:

- A long call calendar spread involves two call options with the same strike price.

- **Longer-Term Call (LEAP):**

The investor buys a call option with a longer time to expiration (e.g., several months or more).

- **Shorter-Term Call:**

The investor sells a call option with a shorter time to expiration (e.g., one month).

2. Same Strike Price:

Both call options in the long call calendar spread have the same strike price.

C. STRATEGY GOALS

1. Time Decay Advantage:

The primary goal is to benefit from the difference in time decay between the longer-term and shorter-term options. The longer-term option experiences less time decay, providing a potential advantage.

2. Capitalize on Stock Price Stability:

The strategy profits when the stock price remains close to the strike price at the expiration of the short-term option.

D. RISKS AND CONSIDERATIONS

1. Limited Profit Potential:

The maximum profit occurs if the stock price is at the strike price at the expiration of the short-term option. Profit potential is limited.

2. Limited Loss Potential:

The maximum loss is limited to the net premium paid to establish the calendar spread. This occurs if the stock price makes a significant move away from the strike price.

3. Implied Volatility Impact:

Changes in implied volatility can impact the value of both the longer-term and shorter-term options. An increase in volatility generally benefits the strategy.

E. EXAMPLE SCENARIO

Suppose a stock is trading at $110. An investor executes a long call calendar spread with the following call options:

- **Longer-Term Call (LEAP):**

Buy a call option with a strike price of $115 expiring in six months for a premium of $8.

- **Shorter-Term Call:**

Sell a call option with a strike price of $115 expiring in one month for a premium of $3.

- **Net Premium Paid:**

The net premium paid is $5 ([$8] - [$3]).

- **Outcomes at Expiration:**

If the stock is at $115 at the expiration of the short-term option, the investor achieves the maximum profit.

If the stock deviates from $115, the profit decreases, reaching a maximum loss if the stock makes a significant move away from the strike price.

F. WHEN TO USE

- **Expectation of Stock Price Stability:**

Long call calendar spreads are effective when an investor expects the underlying stock to remain relatively stable in the short term.

- **Benefiting from Time Decay:**

This strategy is suitable when an investor wants to take advantage of time decay and capitalize on the difference in expiration dates between the longer-term and shorter-term options.

G. STRATEGY ADJUSTMENT

- **Rolling the Short Option:**

As the short option approaches expiration, investors might consider closing it and selling another short-term call option with a later expiration date to extend the strategy.

The long call calendar spread is a strategy designed to capitalize on time decay while maintaining a limited-risk profile. Traders employing this strategy expect the stock to remain close to a specific price and benefit from the difference in time decay between the longer-term and shorter-term options. Careful consideration of market conditions and potential price movements is crucial for successful implementation.

BULL CALL SPREAD

A bull call spread, also known as a debit call spread or a long call spread, is an options trading strategy that involves buying a call option and simultaneously selling another call option with the same expiration date but a higher strike price. This strategy is used when an investor has a moderately bullish outlook on the underlying asset.

Example: Suppose a stock is trading at $50. An investor executes a bull call spread by buying a call option with a strike price of $45 and selling a call option with a strike price of $55, both expiring in one month.

B. Key Components:

1. Call Options:

- A bull call spread involves two call options with the same expiration date.

- **Lower Strike Call (Long Call):**

    o The investor buys a call option with a lower strike price, providing the right to purchase the underlying asset at that price.

- **Higher Strike Call (Short Call):**

- The investor simultaneously sells a call option with a higher strike price, obligating them to sell the underlying asset at that price if the option is exercised.

2. Same Expiration Date:

- Both call options in the bull call spread have the same expiration date.

C. STRATEGY GOALS:

1. Capitalize on Moderate Bullish Outlook:

The primary goal is to profit from a moderately bullish move in the underlying asset. The strategy benefits from an increase in the stock price but with limited risk.

2. Limited Risk and Limited Reward:

The strategy has a limited-risk, limited-reward profile. The maximum loss is the initial premium paid for the long call, and the maximum gain occurs if the stock closes at or above the higher strike price at expiration.

D. RISKS AND CONSIDERATIONS:

1. Limited Profit Potential:

The maximum profit occurs if the stock price is at or above the higher strike price at expiration. Profit potential is limited.

2. Limited Loss Potential:

The maximum loss is limited to the net premium paid to establish the bull call spread. This occurs if the stock price is below the lower strike price at expiration.

3. Breakeven Point:

The breakeven point is the stock price equal to the lower strike price plus the net premium paid. Above this point, the strategy is profitable.

E. EXAMPLE SCENARIO:

Suppose a stock is trading at $60. An investor executes a bull call spread with the following call options:

Lower Strike Call (Long Call):

Buy a call option with a strike price of $55 for a premium of $3.

Higher Strike Call (Short Call):

Sell a call option with a strike price of $65 for a premium of $1.

Net Premium Paid:

The net premium paid is $2 ([$3] - [$1]).

Outcomes at Expiration:

If the stock is at $65 or above at expiration, the investor achieves the maximum profit.

If the stock is below $55 at expiration, the investor incurs the maximum loss.

Between $55 and $65, the strategy is profitable but capped at the difference between the strike prices minus the net premium paid.

F. WHEN TO USE:

Moderately Bullish Outlook:

Bull call spreads are effective when an investor has a moderately bullish view on the underlying asset and expects a gradual price increase.

Limited Capital:

This strategy is suitable when an investor wants to participate in a bullish move with limited capital, as the initial premium paid is lower compared to buying a call option outright.

G. STRATEGY ADJUSTMENT:

- **Rolling the Short Call:**

If the stock price approaches or exceeds the higher strike price, investors might consider rolling the short call to a higher strike or a later expiration date to extend the strategy.

The bull call spread is a strategy designed to capitalize on a moderate bullish move in the underlying asset while maintaining a limited-risk profile. Traders employing this strategy aim to benefit from the potential upside while mitigating the cost through the sale of a higher strike call option. Thorough analysis of market conditions and potential price movements is essential for successful implementation.

BEAR PUT SPREAD

1. Concept:

A bear put spread, also known as a debit put spread or a long put spread, is an options trading strategy that involves buying a put option and simultaneously selling another put option with the same expiration date but a lower strike price. This strategy is employed when an investor has a moderctely bearish outlook on the underlying asset.

Example: Suppose a stock is trading at $60. An investor executes a bear put spread by buying a put option with a strike price of $65 and selling a put option with a strike price of $55, both expiring in one month.

B. KEY COMPONENTS:

1. PUT OPTIONS:

A bear put spread involves two put options with the same expiration date.

Higher Strike Put (Long Put):

The investor buys a put option with a higher strike price, providing the right to sell the underlying asset at that price.

Lower Strike Put (Short Put):

The investor simultaneously sells a put option with a lower strike price, obligating them to buy the underlying asset at that price if the option is exercised.

SAME EXPIRATION DATE:

Both put options in the bear put spread have the same expiration date.

C. STRATEGY GOALS:

1. Capitalize on Moderate Bearish Outlook:

The primary goal is to profit from a moderately bearish move in the underlying asset. The strategy benefits from a decrease in the stock price but with limited risk.

2. Limited Risk and Limited Reward:

The strategy has a limited-risk, limited-reward profile. The maximum loss is the initial premium paid for the long put, and the maximum gain occurs if the stock closes at or below the lower strike price at expiration.

D. RISKS AND CONSIDERATIONS:

1. Limited Profit Potential:

The maximum profit occurs if the stock price is at or below the lower strike price at expiration. Profit potential is limited.

2. Limited Loss Potential:

The maximum loss is limited to the net premium paid to establish the bear put spread. This occurs if the stock price is above the higher strike price at expiration.

3. Breakeven Point:

The breakeven point is the stock price equal to the higher strike price minus the net premium paid. Below this point, the strategy is profitable.

E. Example Scenario:

Suppose a stock is trading at $50. An investor executes a bear put spread with the following put options:

- **Higher Strike Put (Long Put):**

Buy a put option with a strike price of $55 for a premium of $3.

- **Lower Strike Put (Short Put):**

Sell a put option with a strike price of $45 for a premium of $1.

- **Net Premium Paid:**

The net premium paid is $2 ([$3] - [$1]).

- **Outcomes at Expiration:**

- If the stock is at $45 or below at expiration, the investor achieves the maximum profit.

- If the stock is above $55 at expiration, the investor incurs the maximum loss.

- Between $45 and $55, the strategy is profitable but capped at the difference between the strike prices minus the net premium paid.

F. When to Use:

- **Moderately Bearish Outlook:**

Bear put spreads are effective when an investor has a moderately bearish view on the underlying asset and expects a gradual price decrease.

- **Limited Capital:**

This strategy is suitable when an investor wants to participate in a bearish move with limited capital, as the initial premium paid is lower compared to buying a put option outright.

G. STRATEGY ADJUSTMENT:

- **Rolling the Short Put:**

If the stock price approaches or falls below the lower strike price, investors might consider rolling the short put to a lower strike or a later expiration date to extend the strategy.

The bear put spread is a strategy designed to capitalize on a moderate bearish move in the underlying asset while maintaining a limited-risk profile. Traders employing this strategy aim to benefit from the potential downside while mitigating the cost through the sale of a lower strike put option. Thorough analysis of market conditions and potential price movements is essential for successful implementation.

BEAR CALL SPREAD

A bear call spread, also known as a credit call spread or a short call spread, is an options trading strategy that involves selling a call option and simultaneously buying another call option with the same expiration date but a higher strike price. This strategy is employed when an investor has a moderately bearish outlook on the underlying asset.

Example: Suppose a stock is trading at $70. An investor executes a bear call spread by selling a call option with a strike price of $75 and buying a call option with a strike price of $85, both expiring in one month.

B. KEY COMPONENTS:

1. Call Options:

- A bear call spread involves two call options with the same expiration date.

- **Lower Strike Call (Short Call):**

    - The investor sells a call option with a lower strike price, obligating them to sell the underlying asset at that price if the option is exercised.

- **Higher Strike Call (Long Call):**

- o The investor simultaneously buys a call option with a higher strike price, providing the right to purchase the underlying asset at that price.

2. Same Expiration Date:

- Both call options in the bear call spread have the same expiration date.

C. STRATEGY GOALS:

1. Capitalize on Moderate Bearish Outlook:

The primary goal is to profit from a moderately bearish move in the underlying asset. The strategy benefits from the stock price remaining below the lower strike price.

2. Limited Risk and Limited Reward:

The strategy has a limited-risk, limited-reward profile. The maximum loss occurs if the stock price is above the higher strike price at expiration, and the maximum gain occurs if the stock closes at or below the lower strike price at expiration.

D. RISKS AND CONSIDERATIONS:

1. Limited Profit Potential:

The maximum profit occurs if the stock price is below the lower strike price at expiration. Profit potential is limited.

2. Limited Loss Potential:

The maximum loss is limited to the difference in strike prices minus the net premium received to establish the bear call spread. This occurs if the stock price is above the higher strike price at expiration.

3. Breakeven Point:

The breakeven point is the stock price equal to the lower strike price plus the net premium received. Above this point, the strategy starts incurring losses.

E. EXAMPLE SCENARIO:

Suppose a stock is trading at $80. An investor executes a bear call spread with the following call options:

- **Lower Strike Call (Short Call):**

    - Sell a call option with a strike price of $75 for a premium of $3.

- **Higher Strike Call (Long Call):**

    - Buy a call option with a strike price of $85 for a premium of $1.

- **Net Premium Received:**

    - The net premium received is $2 ([$3] - [$1]).

- **Outcomes at Expiration:**

- o If the stock is at \$75 or below at expiration, the investor achieves the maximum profit.

- o If the stock is above \$85 at expiration, the investor incurs the maximum loss.

- o Between \$75 and \$85, the strategy starts incurring losses.

F. WHEN TO USE:

- **Moderately Bearish Outlook:**

Bear call spreads are effective when an investor has a moderately bearish view on the underlying asset and expects a gradual price decrease.

- **Generating Income:**

This strategy is suitable when an investor wants to generate income through the net premium received while participating in a bearish move.

G. STRATEGY ADJUSTMENT:

- **Rolling the Short Call:**

If the stock price approaches or exceeds the lower strike price, investors might consider rolling the short call to a lower strike or a later expiration date to extend the strategy.

The bear call spread is a strategy designed to capitalize on a moderate bearish move in the underlying asset while maintaining a limited-risk profile. Traders employing this strategy aim to generate income through the net premium received while limiting potential losses. Thorough analysis of market conditions and potential price movements is essential for successful implementation.

BULL PUT SPREAD

A bull put spread, also known as a credit put spread or a short put spread, is an options trading strategy that involves selling a put option and simultaneously buying another put option with the same expiration date but a lower strike price. This strategy is employed when an investor has a moderately bullish outlook on the underlying asset.

Example: Suppose a stock is trading at $50. An investor executes a bull put spread by selling a put option with a strike price of $45 and buying a put option with a strike price of $35, both expiring in one month.

B. KEY COMPONENTS:

1. Put Options:

- A bull put spread involves two put options with the same expirction date.

- **Higher Strike Put (Short Put):**

The investor sells a put option with a higher strike price, obligating them to buy the underlying asset at that price if the option is exercised.

- **Lower Strike Put (Long Put):**

    - The investor simultaneously buys a put option with a lower strike price, providing the right to sell the underlying asset at that price.

2. Same Expiration Date:

- Both put options in the bull put spread have the same expiration date.

C. STRATEGY GOALS:

1. Capitalize on Moderate Bullish Outlook:

The primary goal is to profit from a moderately bullish move in the underlying asset. The strategy benefits from the stock price remaining above the higher strike price.

2. Limited Risk and Limited Reward:

The strategy has a limited-risk, limited-reward profile. The maximum loss occurs if the stock price is below the lower strike price at expiration, and the maximum gain occurs if the stock closes at or above the higher strike price at expiration.

D. RISKS AND CONSIDERATIONS:

1. Limited Profit Potential:

The maximum profit occurs if the stock price is above the higher strike price at expiration. Profit potential is limited.

2. Limited Loss Potential:

The maximum loss is limited to the difference in strike prices minus the net premium received to establish the bull put spread. This occurs if the stock price is below the lower strike price at expiration.

3. Breakeven Point:

The breakeven point is the stock price equal to the higher strike price minus the net premium received. Below this point, the strategy starts incurring losses.

E. EXAMPLE SCENARIO:

Suppose a stock is trading at $40. An investor executes a bull put spread with the following put options:

- **Higher Strike Put (Short Put):**

    - Sell a put option with a strike price of $45 for a premium of $2.

- **Lower Strike Put (Long Put):**

    - Buy a put option with a strike price of $35 for a premium of $1.

- **Net Premium Received:**

    - The net premium received is $1 ([$2] - [$1]).

- **Outcomes at Expiration:**

- o If the stock is at $45 or above at expiration, the investor achieves the maximum profit.

- o If the stock is below $35 at expiration, the investor incurs the maximum loss.

- o Between $35 and $45, the strategy starts incurring losses.

F. WHEN TO USE:

- **Moderately Bullish Outlook:**

Bull put spreads are effective when an investor has a moderately bullish view on the underlying asset and expects a gradual price increase.

- **Generating Income:**

This strategy is suitable when an investor wants to generate income through the net premium received while participating in a bullish move.

G. STRATEGY ADJUSTMENT:

- **Rolling the Short Put:**

If the stock price approaches or falls below the lower strike price, investors might consider rolling the short put to a lower strike or a later expiration date to extend the strategy.

The bull put spread is a strategy designed to capitalize on a moderate bullish move in the underlying asset while maintaining a limited-risk profile. Traders employing this strategy aim to generate income through the net premium received while limiting potential losses. Thorough analysis of market conditions and potential price movements is essential for successful implementation.

COVERED CALL

A. Definition:

A covered call is an options trading strategy that involves holding a long position in an underlying asset, such as stocks, and simultaneously selling (writing) a call option on that same asset. The strategy is considered covered because the investor holds the underlying asset, providing coverage in case the option is exercised.

Example: Suppose an investor owns 100 shares of stock XYZ, currently trading at $50 per share. The investor executes a covered call by selling a call option with a strike price of $55, expiring in one month.

B. KEY COMPONENTS:

1. Underlying Asset:

The investor must own the underlying asset (e.g., stocks) in a quantity equal to the contract size of the call options being sold.

2. Short Call Option:

The investor sells a call option, obligating them to sell the underlying asset at the specified strike price if the option is exercised.

3. Same Expiration Date:

Both the long position in the underlying asset and the short call option have the same expiration date.

C. STRATEGY GOALS:

1. Generate Income:

The primary goal is to generate income through the premium received from selling the call option.

2. Capital Appreciation:

The investor benefits from potential capital appreciation of the underlying asset up to the strike price of the call option.

D. RISKS AND CONSIDERATIONS:

1. Limited Upside:

The potential gain from the underlying asset's price appreciation is limited to the strike price of the call option.

2. Obligation to Sell:

- If the stock price rises above the strike price, the investor may be obligated to sell the underlying asset at a price below its market value.

3. Downside Protection:

- The premium received from selling the call option provides some downside protection, reducing the effective purchase cost of the underlying asset.

E. EXAMPLE SCENARIO:

Suppose an investor owns 100 shares of stock ABC, currently trading at $60 per share. The investor executes a covered call with the following details:

- **Underlying Asset (Stock ABC):**

  - 100 shares at $60 per share.

- **Short Call Option:**

  - Sell one call option with a strike price of $65 for a premium of $3, expiring in one month.

- **Net Premium Received:**

  - The net premium received is $300 ([$3] × [100 shares]).

- **Outcomes at Expiration:**

  - If the stock is below $65 at expiration, the investor keeps the premium and the underlying asset.

  - If the stock is at or above $65 at expiration, the investor may be obligated to sell the stock at $65 per share.

F. WHEN TO USE:

- **Neutral to Moderately Bullish Outlook:**

- o Covered calls are effective when the investor has a neutral to moderately bullish outlook on the underlying asset.

- **Income Generation:**

  - o This strategy is suitable for investors looking to generate additional income from their existing stock holdings.

G. STRATEGY ADJUSTMENT:

- **Rolling the Call:**

If the stock price approaches or exceeds the call's strike price, investors might consider rolling the call to a higher strike or a later expiration date to extend the strategy.

The covered call strategy is a conservative approach that combines holding a long position in an underlying asset with selling a call option. It is popular among income-oriented investors seeking to generate additional cash flow from their stock holdings. Careful consideration of market conditions and potential price movements is crucial for successful implementation.

LONG COMBO

A. Definition:

A long combo, also known as a synthetic long stock or synthetic stock position, is an options trading strategy that mimics the behavior of owning the underlying asset (such as stocks) by combining a long call option and a short put option with the same strike price and expiration date. The strategy is structured to profit from the underlying asset's price appreciation.

Example: Suppose an investor executes a long combo on stock XYZ by buying a call option with a strike price of $50 and simultaneously selling a put option with the same $50 strike price, both expiring in one month.

B. KEY COMPONENTS:

1. Long Call Option:

The investor buys a call option, giving them the right to purchase the underlying asset at the specified strike price.

2. Short Put Option:

The investor sells a put option, obligating them to buy the underlying asset at the specified strike price if the option is exercised.

3. Same Strike Price and Expiration Date:

Both the long call option and the short put option have the same strike price and expiration date.

1. Mimic Long Stock Position:

The primary goal is to replicate the profit and loss characteristics of owning the underlying asset, making the strategy similar to holding a long stock position.

2. Capital Appreciation:

The investor benefits from potential capital appreciation of the underlying asset, as gains from the long call offset losses from the short put.

D. RISKS AND CONSIDERATIONS:

1. Limited Risk:

The maximum loss is limited to the net premium paid to establish the long combo.

2. Unlimited Profit Potential:

The profit potential is theoretically unlimited, as the investor benefits from the underlying asset's price appreciation.

3. Obligation to Buy Stock:

If the stock price falls below the strike price, the investor may be obligated to buy the underlying asset at a price above its market value.

E. EXAMPLE SCENARIO:

Suppose an investor executes a long combo on stock ABC with the following details:

- **Long Call Option:**

    - Buy one call option with a strike price of $60 for a premium of $3, expiring in one month.

- **Short Put Option:**

    - Sell one put option with a strike price of $60 for a premium of $2, expiring in one month.

- **Net Premium Paid/Received:**

    - The net premium paid is $1 ([$3] - [$2]).

- **Outcomes at Expiration:**

    - If the stock is above $60 at expiration, the investor benefits from capital appreciation.

    - If the stock is below $60 at expiration, the investor may be obligated to buy the stock at $60 per share.

F. When to Use:

- **Bullish Outlook:**

A long combo is effective when the investor has a bullish outlook on the underlying asset and expects its price to rise.

- **Low Capital:**

This strategy is suitable for investors seeking a bullish position with lower capital requirements compared to outright stock ownership.

G. STRATEGY ADJUSTMENT:

- **Rolling Options:**

If the stock price approaches or falls below the strike price, investors might consider rolling the options to a lower strike or a later expiration date to extend the strategy.

The long combo is a versatile strategy that allows investors to benefit from a bullish market outlook while having limited risk. By combining a long call option with a short put option, the investor creates a position that mirrors owning the underlying asset. Thorough analysis of market conditions and potential price movements is essential for successful implementation.

COLLAR

A. Definition:

1. Concept:

A collar is an options trading strategy that involves holding a long position in an underlying asset, such as stocks, and simultaneously buying a protective put option while selling a covered call option. This strategy is designed to provide downside protection to the long position while capping potential gains.

Example: Suppose an investor owns 100 shares of stock XYZ, currently trading at $70 per share. The investor executes a collar by buying a put option with a strike price of $65 and selling a call option with a strike price of $75, both expiring in one month.

B. Key Components:

1. Underlying Asset:

The investor must own the underlying asset (e.g., stocks) in a quantity equal to the contract size of the call options being sold.

2. Protective Put Option:

The investor buys a put option, providing downside protection by allowing them to sell the underlying asset at the specified strike price if its price falls.

3. Covered Call Option:

The investor sells a call option, generating income and obligating them to sell the underlying asset at the specified strike price if the option is exercised.

4. Same Expiration Date:

Both the protective put option and the covered call option have the same expiration date.

C. STRATEGY GOALS:

1. Downside Protection:

The primary goal is to limit potential losses on the underlying asset by owning a protective put option.

2. Income Generation:

The investor generates income through the premium received from selling the covered call option.

3. Capped Gains:

Gains on the underlying asset are capped due to the obligation to sell at the covered call's strike price.

D. Risks and Considerations:

1. Limited Upside:

The potential gain from the underlying asset's price appreciation is limited to the covered call's strike price.

2. Limited Downside:

The maximum loss is limited to the difference between the purchase price of the underlying asset and the put option's strike price.

3. Call Exercise Risk:

If the stock price rises above the covered call's strike price, the investor may be obligated to sell the underlying asset at a price below its market value.

E. Example Scenario:

Suppose an investor owns 100 shares of stock ABC, currently trading at $80 per share. The investor executes a collar with the following details:

- **Underlying Asset (Stock ABC):**
    - 100 shares at $80 per share.

- **Protective Put Option:**
    - Buy one put option with a strike price of $75 for a premium of $2, expiring in one month.

- **Covered Call Option:**
    - Sell one call option with a strike price of $85 for a premium of $3, expiring in one month.

- **Net Premium Paid/Received:**
    - The net premium received is $1 ([$3] - [$2]).

- **Outcomes at Expiration:**
  - If the stock is above $85 at expiration, the investor may be obligated to sell the stock at $85 per share.
  - If the stock is below $75 at expiration, the investor can exercise the put option to sell the stock at $75 per share.

F. WHEN TO USE:

- **Neutral to Moderately Bullish Outlook with Downside Concerns:**

A collar is effective when the investor has a neutral to moderately bullish outlook on the underlying asset but wants downside protection.

- **Generating Income:**

This strategy is suitable for investors looking to generate income through the net premium received while protecting their long position.

G. STRATEGY ADJUSTMENT:

- **Adjusting Strike Prices:**

Investors can adjust the strike prices of the put and call options based on market conditions and their risk tolerance.

The collar strategy is a conservative approach that combines holding a long position in an underlying asset with the simultaneous purchase of a protective put and the sale of a covered call. It is designed to provide downside protection while generating income. Careful consideration of market conditions and potential price movements is crucial for successful implementation.

LONG CALL BUTTERFLY

A. Definition:

A long call butterfly, also known as a call butterfly spread, is an options trading strategy that involves buying one lower strike call option, selling two middle strike call options, and buying one higher strike call option. The strikes are evenly spaced, creating a profit and loss profile that resembles a butterfly. This strategy is used when an investor expects minimal price movement in the underlying asset.

Example: Suppose a stock is trading at $50. An investor executes a long call butterfly by:

- Buying one call option with a strike price of $45.

- Selling two call options with a strike price of $50.

- Buying one call option with a strike price of $55.

B. KEY COMPONENTS:

1. Call Options:

- In a long call butterfly, four call options are involved with three different strike prices.

- **Lower Strike Call (Long Call):**

- o The investor buys one call option with the lowest strike price.

- • **Middle Strike Calls (Short Calls):**

  - o The investor sells two call options with the middle strike price.

- • **Higher Strike Call (Long Call):**

  - o The investor buys one call option with the highest strike price.

2. Same Expiration Date:

- • All call options in the long call butterfly have the same expiration date.

C. STRATEGY GOALS:

1. Limited Risk, Limited Reward:

The primary goal is to achieve a low-cost, limited-risk strategy with a capped profit potential.

2. Neutral Outlook:

The strategy profits the most when the underlying asset's price remains close to the middle strike price, reflecting a neutral outlook.

D. RISKS AND CONSIDERATIONS:

1. Maximum Loss:

The maximum loss occurs if the stock price is below the lower strike or above the higher strike at expiration, and it is limited to the initial premium paid to establish the butterfly.

2. Maximum Gain:

The maximum gain occurs if the stock price is at the middle strike at expiration. It is limited and represents the difference between the middle and lower strike prices, minus the initial premium paid.

3. Breakeven Points:

There are two breakeven points, which occur when the stock price is equal to the lower strike plus the net premium paid and the higher strike minus the net premium paid.

E. Example Scenario:

Suppose an investor executes a long call butterfly on stock ABC with the following call options:

- **Lower Strike Call (Long Call):**

    - Buy one call option with a strike price of $45 for a premium of $2.

- **Middle Strike Calls (Short Calls):**

    - Sell two call options with a strike price of $50 for a premium of $1 each.

- **Higher Strike Call (Long Call):**

- o Buy one call option with a strike price of $55 for a premium of $2.

- **Net Premium Paid/Received:**

  - o The net premium paid is $1 ([$2 + $2] - [$1 + $1]).

- **Outcomes at Expiration:**

  - o Maximum loss if the stock is below $45 or above $55.

  - o Maximum gain if the stock is at $50.

  - o Profit potential between $46 and $49 and between $51 and $54.

F. WHEN TO USE:

- **Expectation of Low Volatility:**

A long call butterfly is effective when an investor expects minimal price movement in the underlying asset.

- **Low-Cost Strategy:**

This strategy is suitable when seeking a low-cost, limited-risk trade with a defined profit and loss profile.

G. STRATEGY ADJUSTMENT:

- **Rolling or Adjusting Strikes:**

Depending on market conditions, investors may consider rolling the position or adjusting the strike prices to adapt to changing price dynamics.

The long call butterfly is a neutral options strategy that profits from minimal price movement in the underlying asset. It offers a limited-risk, limited-reward profile, making it suitable for traders expecting low volatility in the near term. Careful consideration of market conditions and potential price movements is essential for successful implementation.

LONG CALL CALENDER SPREAD

A. Definition:

A long call calendar spread, also known as a time spread or horizontal spread, is an options trading strategy that involves buying a longer-term call option and simultaneously selling a shorter-term call option with the same strike price. This strategy aims to profit from the difference in time decay between the two options while maintaining a bullish outlook.

Example: Suppose a stock is trading at $60. An investor executes a long call calendar spread by:

- Buying a call option with a strike price of $60 and an expiration date in three months.

- Simultaneously selling a call option with the same $60 strike price and an expiration date in one month.

B. KEY COMPONENTS:

1. Call Options:

- In a long call calendar spread, two call options are involved with the same strike price.

- **Longer-Term Call (Long Call):**

  - The investor buys a call option with a longer expiration date.

- **Shorter-Term Call (Short Call):**

    - The investor sells a call option with a shorter expiration date.

2. Same Strike Price:

- Both call options in the long call calendar spread have the same strike price.

C. STRATEGY GOALS:

1. Time Decay Profit:

The primary goal is to profit from the time decay of the short-term call option, which accelerates as it approaches expiration.

2. Limited Risk:

The maximum loss is limited to the initial premium paid to establish the calendar spread.

3. Bullish Outlook:

The strategy benefits from a gradual increase in the underlying asset's price, but it can also be profitable in a stable market.

D. RISKS AND CONSIDERATIONS:

1. Maximum Loss:

The maximum loss occurs if the stock price is at or below the strike price at the expiration of the short-term call option.

2. Maximum Gain:

The maximum gain occurs if the stock price is at the strike price at the expiration of the short-term call option, and it is limited.

3. Breakeven Points:

There are two breakeven points. One is when the stock price is equal to the strike price plus the net premium paid for the calendar spread. The other is when the stock price is below the strike price at the expiration of the short-term call option.

E. EXAMPLE SCENARIO:

Suppose an investor executes a long call calendar spread on stock ABC with the following call options:

- **Longer-Term Call (Long Call):**

    - Buy one call option with a strike price of $65 and an expiration date in three months for a premium of $4.

- **Shorter-Term Call (Short Call):**

    - Sell one call option with a strike price of $65 and an expiration date in one month for a premium of $2.

- **Net Premium Paid/Received:**

    - The net premium paid is $2 ([$4] - [$2]).

- **Outcomes at Expiration:**

    - Maximum loss if the stock is at or below $65 at the expiration of the short-term call option.

    - Maximum gain if the stock is at $65 at the expiration of the short-term call option.

    - Profit potential if the stock is between $65 and $69 (strike price plus net premium paid).

F. WHEN TO USE:

- **Expectation of Low Volatility:**

A long call calendar spread is effective when an investor expects low short-term volatility but anticipates gradual price movement in the longer term.

- **Time Decay Advantage:**

This strategy is suitable for traders seeking to benefit from time decay while maintaining a bullish outlook.

G. STRATEGY ADJUSTMENT:

- **Rolling Options:**

As the short-term call option approaches expiration, investors may consider rolling it to a later expiration date to extend the time decay advantage.

The long call calendar spread is a strategy that leverages time decay to potentially generate profits. It is suitable for investors anticipating low short-term volatility and a gradual increase in the underlying asset's price. Careful consideration of market conditions and option pricing dynamics is essential for successful implementation.

IRON CONDOR

A. Definition:

An iron condor is an advanced options trading strategy that involves the simultaneous use of both a bear call spread and a bull put spread. This strategy is used when an investor expects minimal price movement in the underlying asset, creating a range-bound scenario.

Example: Suppose a stock is trading at $70. An investor executes an iron condor by:

- Selling a call option with a strike price of $75.

- Buying a call option with a higher strike price of $80.

- Selling a put option with a strike price of $65.

- Buying a put option with a lower strike price of $60.

B. KEY COMPONENTS:

1. CALL OPTIONS:

- The iron condor involves two call spreads.

- **Bear Call Spread:**

    o Sell one call option with a lower strike price.

- o   Buy one call option with a higher strike price.

PUT OPTIONS:

- • The iron condor involves two put spreads.

- • **Bull Put Spread:**

  - o   Sell one put option with a higher strike price.

  - o   Buy one put option with a lower strike price.

C. STRATEGY GOALS:

1. Profit from Low Volatility:

The primary goal is to profit from minimal price movement in the underlying asset, resulting in the options expiring out of the money.

2. Limited Risk, Limited Reward:

The strategy has a defined risk and reward profile, providing a range within which the investor profits.

D. RISKS AND CONSIDERATIONS:

1. Maximum Loss:

The maximum loss occurs if the stock price is at or above the higher strike price of the call spread or at or below the lower strike price of the put spread.

2. Maximum Gain:

The maximum gain occurs if the stock price is between the two strike prices of the call spread and the two strike prices of the put spread at expiration.

3. Breakeven Points:

There are two breakeven points, which occur when the stock price is equal to the lower strike price of the put spread plus the net premium received and the higher strike price of the call spread minus the net premium received.

E. EXAMPLE SCENARIO:

Suppose an investor executes an iron condor on stock ABC with the following options:

- **Bear Call Spread:**

    o   Sell one call option with a strike price of $75 for a premium of $2.

    o   Buy one call option with a strike price of $80 for a premium of $1.

- **Bull Put Spread:**

    o   Sell one put option with a strike price of $65 for a premium of $2.

    o   Buy one put option with a strike price of $60 for a premium of $1.

- **Net Premium Received/Paid:**

- o The net premium received is $2 - $1 + $2 - $1 = $2.

- **Outcomes at Expiration:**

  - o Maximum loss if the stock is at or above $80 or at or below $60.

  - o Maximum gain if the stock is between $65 and $75.

F. WHEN TO USE:

- **Expectation of Low Volatility:**

An iron condor is effective when an investor expects low volatility and a sideways or range-bound movement in the underlying asset.

- **Income Generation:**

This strategy is suitable for generating income through the net premium received.

G. STRATEGY ADJUSTMENT:

- **Rolling Options:**

If the stock price approaches one of the breakeven points, investors may consider rolling the position to a later expiration date or adjusting the strike prices to manage risk.

The iron condor is a popular strategy for traders expecting low volatility and a relatively stable market environment. It offers a defined risk and reward profile and is commonly used for income generation. Careful consideration of market conditions and potential price movements is essential for successful implementation.

DOUBLE DIAGONAL

A. Definition:

A double diagonal spread is an advanced options trading strategy that combines elements of both a long call diagonal spread and a long put diagonal spread. It involves buying and selling options with different strike prices and expiration dates to capitalize on time decay and volatility changes. This strategy is suitable for investors expecting moderate price movement in the underlying asset.

Example: Suppose a stock is trading at $75. An investor executes a double diagonal spread by:

- Buying a longer-term call option with a strike price of $70.

- Selling a near-term call option with a higher strike price of $80.

- Buying a longer-term put option with a strike price of $80.

- Selling a near-term put option with a lower strike price of $70.

B. KEY COMPONENTS:

1. Call Options:

- The double diagonal spread involves two call diagonal spreads.

- **Long Call Diagonal Spread:**

    o Buy a longer-term call option with a lower strike price.

    o Sell a near-term call option with a higher strike price.

2. Put Options:

- The double diagonal spread involves two put diagonal spreads.

- **Long Put Diagonal Spread:**

    o Buy a longer-term put option with a higher strike price.

    o Sell a near-term put option with a lower strike price.

C. STRATEGY GOALS:

1. Leverage Time Decay:

The primary goal is to profit from time decay, as the options with shorter expiration dates decay faster than those with longer expiration dates.

2. Benefit from Volatility Changes:

The strategy can benefit from changes in implied volatility, especially if it increases.

D. RISKS AND CONSIDERATIONS:

1. Maximum Loss:

The maximum loss occurs if the stock price is at or above the higher strike price of the call spread or at or below the lower strike price of the put spread.

2. Maximum Gain:

The maximum gain occurs if the stock price is close to the strike prices of both the call and put spreads at expiration.

3. Breakeven Points:

There are two breakeven points, one for the call spread and one for the put spread, depending on the net premium paid or received.

E. EXAMPLE SCENARIO:

Suppose an investor executes a double diagonal spread on stock ABC with the following options:

- **Long Call Diagonal Spread:**

    - Buy a longer-term call option with a strike price of $70 for a premium of $4.

    - Sell a near-term call option with a strike price of $80 for a premium of $2.

- **Long Put Diagonal Spread:**

- o Buy a longer-term put option with a strike price of $80 for a premium of $5.

- o Sell a near-term put option with a strike price of $70 for a premium of $3.

- **Net Premium Paid/Received:**

  - o The net premium paid or received is the sum of the individual premiums in each spread.

- **Outcomes at Expiration:**

  - o Maximum loss if the stock is at or above $80 or at or below $70.

  - o Maximum gain if the stock is close to the $75 range, between the two strike prices.

F. WHEN TO USE:

- **Expectation of Moderate Price Movement:**

A double diagonal spread is effective when an investor expects moderate price movement in the underlying asset.

- **Leveraging Time Decay:**

This strategy is suitable for leveraging time decay by utilizing options with different expiration dates.

G. Strategy Adjustment:

- **Rolling or Adjusting Strikes:**

Depending on market conditions, investors may consider rolling the position or adjusting the strike prices to adapt to changing dynamics.

The double diagonal spread is a complex strategy that benefits from time decay and volatility changes. It provides a range within which the investor can profit and is suitable for those anticipating moderate price movement in the underlying asset. Thorough analysis of market conditions and option pricing dynamics is essential for successful implementation.

CHRISTMAS TREE SPREAD

A Christmas tree spread is an advanced options trading strategy that involves buying and selling multiple options with different strike prices and expiration dates. This strategy is named for its visual resemblance to a Christmas tree when mapped on an options chain. It is designed to capitalize on both time decay and potential price movements in the underlying asset.

Example: Suppose a stock is trading at $80. An investor executes a Christmas tree spread by:

- Buying a call option with a near-term expiration date and a lower strike price (e.g., $75).

- Selling multiple call options with the same expiration date but higher strike prices (e.g., $80, $85, $90).

B. KEY COMPONENTS:

1. Call Options:

- The Christmas tree spread involves a combination of long and short call options with different strike prices.

- **Long Call Option:**

    o Buy a call option with a lower strike price and a near-term expiration date.

- **Short Call Options:**

  - Sell multiple call options with the same expiration date but higher strike prices.

C. STRATEGY GOALS:

1. Leverage Time Decay:

- The primary goal is to benefit from time decay by selling multiple call options with higher strike prices.

2. Capitalize on Price Movement:

- The strategy can profit from price movements if the underlying asset's price reaches or surpasses the sold call options' strike prices.

D. RISKS AND CONSIDERATIONS:

1. Maximum Loss:

The maximum loss occurs if the stock price is above the highest strike price of the sold call options at expiration.

2. Maximum Gain:

The maximum gain occurs if the stock price is at or above the highest strike price of the sold call options at expiration.

3. Breakeven Points:

The breakeven points depend on the net premium paid or received and the stock price at expiration.

E. EXAMPLE SCENARIO:

Suppose an investor executes a Christmas tree spread on stock ABC with the following call options:

- **Long Call Option:**

    - Buy one call option with a strike price of $75 for a premium of $3 and an expiration date in one month.

- **Short Call Options:**

    - Sell three call options with strike prices of $80, $85, and $90, each for a premium of $1 and with the same expiration date.

- **Net Premium Paid/Received:**

    - The net premium paid or received is the difference between the premium paid for the long call and the total premium received for the short call options.

- **Outcomes at Expiration:**

    - Maximum loss if the stock is above $90 at expiration.

- o Maximum gain if the stock is at or above $90 at expiration.

- o Profit potential if the stock is between $76 and $89.

F. WHEN TO USE:

- **Expectation of Moderate Price Movement:**

A Christmas tree spread is effective when an investor expects moderate price movement in the underlying asset.

- **Leveraging Time Decay:**

This strategy is suitable for leveraging time decay by selling multiple call options.

G. STRATEGY ADJUSTMENT:

- **Rolling or Adjusting Strikes:**

Depending on market conditions, investors may consider rolling the position or adjusting the strike prices to manage risk.

The Christmas tree spread is a complex strategy that combines elements of time decay and potential price movements. It offers a defined risk and reward profile and is suitable for traders anticipating moderate price movement in the underlying asset. Thorough analysis of market conditions and option pricing dynamics is essential for successful implementation.

SYNTHETIC LONG STOCK

A synthetic long stock is an options trading strategy that replicates the payoff and risk profile of owning the underlying stock. It involves creating a position using a combination of options contracts to mimic the behavior of being long (owning) the stock. This strategy is useful when an investor wants to benefit from the price appreciation of the underlying asset without actually buying the stock.

Example: Suppose a stock is trading at $50. An investor executes a synthetic long stock by:

- Buying a call option with a strike price of $50.

- Simultaneously selling a put option with the same strike price of $50.

B. KEY COMPONENTS:

1. Call Option:

- In a synthetic long stock, the investor buys a call option with a specific strike price.

2. Put Option:

- Simultaneously, the investor sells a put option with the same strike price as the call option.

C. STRATEGY GOALS:

1. Replicate Stock Ownership:

- The primary goal is to replicate the payoff and risk characteristics of owning the underlying stock.

2. Benefit from Price Appreciation:

- The strategy profits from an increase in the underlying asset's price.

D. RISKS AND CONSIDERATIONS:

1. Limited Risk:

The risk is limited to the net premium paid to establish the synthetic long stock position.

2. Unlimited Profit Potential:

The profit potential is theoretically unlimited as the stock price can rise significantly.

3. Breakeven Point:

The breakeven point is the strike price of the call option plus the net premium paid.

E. EXAMPLE SCENARIO:

Suppose an investor executes a synthetic long stock on stock ABC with the following options:

- **Call Option:**

Buy one call option with a strike price of $50 for a premium of $2 and an expiration date in one month.

- **Put Option:**

Simultaneously, sell one put option with a strike price of $50 for a premium of $1 and with the same expiration date.

- **Net Premium Paid/Received:**

    o   The net premium paid is $2 - $1 = $1.

- **Outcomes at Expiration:**

    o   Maximum loss of $1 if the stock is below $50 at expiration.

    o   Maximum gain is theoretically unlimited if the stock appreciates significantly.

F. WHEN TO USE:

- **Bullish Outlook:**

A synthetic long stock is effective when the investor has a bullish outlook on the underlying asset.

- **Limited Capital:**

This strategy is suitable when an investor has limited capital but wants to participate in potential stock price appreciation.

G. STRATEGY ADJUSTMENT:

- **Rolling Options:**

Depending on market conditions, investors may consider rolling the position or adjusting the strike prices to adapt to changing dynamics.

The synthetic long stock strategy is a cost-effective way to replicate stock ownership using options. It is commonly employed when an investor expects the underlying asset's price to rise and wants to benefit from this without directly purchasing the stock. Thorough analysis of market conditions and option pricing dynamics is essential for successful implementation.

OPTION BUYING

Option buying, or long options, involves purchasing the right, but not the obligation, to buy or sell an underlying asset at a predetermined price (strike price) within a specified timeframe (expiration date). Despite the upfront cost associated with buying options, this strategy offers several compelling advantages:

1. **Limited Risk, Unlimited Potential Reward**: Unlike other trading strategies with unlimited downside risk, option buying offers limited risk, as the maximum loss is capped at the premium paid. Meanwhile, the profit potential remains theoretically unlimited, allowing traders to benefit from significant market moves.

2. **Enhanced Leverage**: Option buying enables traders to control a larger position in the underlying asset with a relatively small investment, amplifying potential returns.

3. **Strategic Flexibility**: Long options can be utilized in various market conditions, including bullish, bearish, or even neutral outlooks, offering versatility to traders.

Strategies for Success

Successful option buying requires a nuanced understanding of market dynamics and a strategic approach tailored to individual trading objectives. Let's explore some popular option buying strategies with practical examples:

1. **Long Call Options**: This strategy involves purchasing call options to profit from upward price movements in the underlying asset. For instance, if you're bullish on Company ABC, currently trading at $50 per share, you could buy a call option with a strike price of $55 and an expiration date one month away for a premium of $3 per share. If the stock price rises above $58 ($55 strike price + $3 premium), you start to profit.

2. **Long Put Options**: Conversely, long put options are used to profit from downward price movements in the underlying asset. Suppose you anticipate a bearish trend in Company XYZ, currently trading at $70 per share. You could buy a put option with a strike price of $65 and an expiration date one month away for a premium of $4 per share. If the stock price drops below $61 ($65 strike price - $4 premium), you begin to profit.

3. **Long Straddle Options**: This strategy involves simultaneously purchasing both call and put options with the same strike price and expiration date. For example, if you expect significant

volatility in the market following an earnings announcement for Company DEF, currently trading at $80 per share, you could buy a straddle option with a strike price of $80 and an expiration date one month away. If the stock experiences substantial price movements in either direction, you stand to profit from the increased volatility.

Risk Management Techniques

While option buying offers compelling opportunities, prudent risk management is essential to mitigate potential losses. Here are some risk management techniques to consider:

1. **Position Sizing**: Limit the size of option buying positions to a fraction of your total capital to avoid overexposure to risk.

2. **Setting Stop Loss Orders**: Consider implementing stop loss orders to exit positions if losses exceed predetermined thresholds, protecting capital from significant drawdowns.

3. **Diversification**: Diversify option buying strategies across different underlying assets, strike prices, and expiration dates to spread risk and enhance overall portfolio stability.

In the following chapters we will discuss some of the commonly used option buying strategies

PRICE ACTION TRADING

Price action trading involves making trading decisions based on the actual price movements of an asset rather than relying on traditional indicators or technical analysis. When applying price action principles to option buying, traders often focus on chart patterns, key support and resistance levels, and trend analysis. Here are some considerations when using price action for option buying:

1. Candlestick Patterns:

Engulfing Patterns, Doji, and Hammers: Observing these candlestick patterns can provide insights into potential reversals or continuations in price trends.

2. Support and Resistance Levels:

Key Price Levels: Identify significant support and resistance levels on the price chart. These levels can act as potential entry or exit points for option trades.

3. Trend Analysis:

Identifying Trends: Determine the prevailing trend using trendlines or moving averages. Options might be bought in the direction of the trend, anticipating continued momentum.

BREAKOUTS AND BREAKDOWNS:

Breakout Strategies: Look for breakouts above resistance or breakdowns below support. Option buying can be considered when the price breaks out, anticipating a strong move.

VOLATILITY CONSIDERATIONS:

Volatility Squeeze: Identify periods of low volatility (squeeze) on the price chart. Options are often cheaper during low volatility, and traders may anticipate a subsequent volatility expansion.

MULTIPLE TIME FRAME ANALYSIS:

Confirmation from Different Time Frames: Confirm price action signals on your chosen time frame with those from higher and lower time frames to increase the reliability of the setup.

NEWS AND EVENTS:

Economic Events and News Releases: Be aware of upcoming economic events or news releases that might impact the underlying asset's price. Option buying strategies can be adapted based on expectations surrounding these events.

RISK MANAGEMENT

Setting Stop-Loss and Take-Profit Levels: Establish clear risk management rules, including setting stop-loss levels based on technical levels or volatility considerations.

CHART PATTERNS:

- **Head and Shoulders, Double Tops/Bottoms:** Recognize classical chart patterns that may signal reversals or continuations. Option buying decisions can be made based on the implications of these patterns.

CONFIRMATION INDICATORS

Volume Analysis: Confirm price movements with volume analysis. A surge in volume can provide confirmation of a strong price move.

Implied Volatility:

Volatility Contraction and Expansion: Consider option buying during periods of low implied volatility, anticipating a potential volatility expansion.

PSYCHOLOGICAL LEVELS

Round Numbers: Psychological levels, such as round numbers, can act as significant support or resistance levels. Option buying decisions might be influenced by price action around these levels.

Divergence Analysis:

Price vs. Indicators: Look for divergences between price action and technical indicators, which may signal potential reversals.

IMPORTANT CONSIDERATIONS:

Learning and Experience: Successful price action trading requires a solid understanding of chart patterns and market dynamics. Continuous learning and experience are crucial.

Combining with Fundamental Analysis: Consider combining price action analysis with fundamental analysis for a more comprehensive view of the market.

FIBONACCI RETRACEMENT STRATEGY

Fibonacci Retracement Strategy

Concept:

The Fibonacci Retracement Strategy involves using Fibonacci retracement levels to identify potential reversal points in the price of an asset.

Execution:

- Buy Call options at key Fibonacci support levels.

- Buy Put options at key Fibonacci resistance levels.

Considerations:

- Confirm signals with other technical indicators or price action patterns.

- Align with broader market trends for increased reliability.

Execution Steps:

1. **Identify Trend:** Determine the prevailing trend in the market (uptrend or downtrend).

2. **Draw Fibonacci Levels:** Identify significant price swings within the trend and draw Fibonacci retracement levels. Common levels include 38.2%, 50%, and 61.8%.

3. **Wait for Retracement:** Wait for the price to retrace to one of the Fibonacci levels.

4. **Confirm with Indicators:** Confirm the retracement with other technical indicators such as RSI or MACD. Look for convergence of signals.

5. **Options Execution:** If the price confirms a bounce from a Fibonacci support level, consider buying Call options. If it confirms resistance at a Fibonacci level, consider buying Put options.

6. **Risk Management:** Set stop-loss orders to manage downside risk. Adjust position sizes based on risk tolerance.

Considerations:

- Fibonacci retracement levels are more effective when combined with other technical analysis tools.

- Monitor broader market conditions and news events that may impact the asset.

RANGE BREAKOUT STRATEGY

Range Breakout Overview:

The Range Breakout Strategy is employed when traders anticipate a significant price movement after an extended period of price consolidation within a defined range.

Execution:

1. **Identify the Range:**

Identify a well-defined price range where the underlying asset has been trading within a specified period. This range is characterized by a clear upper resistance level and a lower support level.

2. **Confirmation of Breakout:**

Wait for the price to break decisively above the upper resistance level or below the lower support level.

3. **Trigger for Trade:**

Initiate a trade in the direction of the breakout:

- **Breakout to the Upside:**
  - Consider buying Call options or executing bullish strategies.

- **Breakout to the Downside:**

- Consider buying Put options or executing bearish strategies.

Considerations:

1. Confirmation Signals:

Use additional technical indicators, chart patterns, or volume analysis to confirm the breakout signals.

2. Volatility Consideration:

Expect higher volatility during the breakout period. Adjust position sizes accordingly.

3. Time Frame Selection:

Choose an appropriate time frame for the breakout, considering the trading horizon and overall market conditions.

4. Risk Management:

Implement risk management practices, including setting stop-loss orders, to control potential losses.

Example Scenario:

- **Range: $95 - $105**

- **Breakout: Price rises above $105**

- **Trade Execution:**
  - Buy Call options or execute bullish strategies.

- **Outcome:**

  - If the breakout is successful, the underlying asset's price may continue rising, leading to potential profits.

Strategy Summary:

The Range Breakout Strategy capitalizes on significant price movements following a prolonged period of consolidation. Traders aim to catch a trend early by initiating options positions in the direction of the breakout. This strategy requires careful analysis, confirmation signals, and effective risk management to navigate potential market volatility.

PIVOT POINTS STRATEGY

Pivot points are technical indicators used to identify potential support and resistance levels based on the previous day's price action. Traders use these levels to make informed decisions about potential entry and exit points.

EXECUTION:

1. **Calculation of Pivot Points:**

Calculate the pivot point and associated support and resistance levels using the high, low, and close prices from the previous trading day.

2. **Identification of Key Levels:**

Identify key levels, including the pivot point, support levels, and resistance levels.

3. **Market Conditions Assessment:**

Assess current market conditions in relation to the pivot points. Look for potential areas where the price might reverse or continue its trend.

4. **Trigger for Trade:**

Based on the assessment, initiate an options trade:

- **Call Options:**

- Consider buying Call options if the price is bouncing off a support level or breaking above a resistance level.

- **Put Options:**

  - Consider buying Put options if the price is rejecting a resistance level or breaking below a support level.

CONSIDERATIONS:

1. **Confirmation with Other Indicators:**

Confirm pivot points signals with other technical indicators, such as moving averages or trendlines, for added reliability.

2. **Time Frame Selection:**

Choose an appropriate time frame for the analysis, considering the trading horizon and overall market conditions.

3. **Volatility Analysis:**

Consider volatility levels when interpreting pivot points. Higher volatility may impact the effectiveness of support and resistance levels.

4. **Risk Management:**

Implement risk management practices, including setting stop-loss orders, to control potential losses.

EXAMPLE SCENARIO:

- **Pivot Point: $100**

- **Support Levels: $95, $90**

- **Resistance Levels: $105, $110**

Trade Execution:

a) Buy Call options if the price bounces off the support level at $95.
b) Buy Put options if the price fails to break above the resistance level at $105.

- **Outcome:**

If the trade is successful, the underlying asset's price may follow the expected trend, leading to potential profits.

Strategy Summary:

The Pivot Points Strategy for Option Buying utilizes key support and resistance levels derived from pivot points to make informed options trading decisions.

MACD CROSSOVER STRATEGY

Concept:

The MACD (Moving Average Convergence Divergence) Crossover Strategy is a trend-following strategy that uses the MACD indicator to identify potential trend reversals and entry points in the market.

EXECUTION:

BUY CALL OPTIONS ON BULLISH CROSSOVER:

- Look for a bullish crossover, where the MACD line crosses above the Signal line.

- Consider buying Call options when this crossover occurs.

BUY PUT OPTIONS ON BEARISH CROSSOVER:

- Look for a bearish crossover, where the MACD line crosses below the Signal line.

- Consider buying Put options when this crossover occurs.

CONSIDERATIONS:

1. **Divergence Confirmation:**

Confirm MACD signals with price action divergence. If prices are making new highs while the MACD is not, or vice versa, it may strengthen the signal.

2. **Time Frame Adjustments:**

Adjust the time frame of the MACD indicator based on the desired trading horizon. Shorter time frames may be suitable for day trading, while longer time frames may be suitable for swing trading.

3. **Additional Confirmation Indicators:**

Use other technical indicators or chart patterns to confirm MACD signals for a more robust trading decision.

4. **Risk Management:**

Implement risk management practices, including setting stop-loss orders, to control potential losses.

EXECUTION STEPS:

1. **Plot MACD Indicator:**

   o Plot the MACD indicator on the price chart.

2. **Identify Crossovers:**

- o Look for crossovers between the MACD line and the Signal line.

3. **Confirm Market Conditions:**

   - o Confirm the overall market conditions and trend direction.

4. **Execute Options Trade:**

   - o Execute a Call option trade on a bullish crossover.

   - o Execute a Put option trade on a bearish crossover.

5. **Monitor and Adjust:**

   - o Monitor the trade and be prepared to adjust or exit based on changing market conditions.

The MACD Crossover Strategy is a popular and widely used approach for identifying potential trend reversals and entry points. Traders should use this strategy in conjunction with other analysis tools and adapt it to their risk tolerance and trading style.

RSI OVERBOUGHT/OVERSOLD STRATEGY

The RSI (Relative Strength Index) Overbought/Oversold Strategy is a momentum-based strategy that uses the RSI indicator to identify potential reversal points in an asset's price.

EXECUTION:

Buy Call Options in Oversold Conditions:

- o When the RSI falls below a certain threshold (typically 30), it indicates oversold conditions, suggesting a potential buying opportunity. Consider buying Call options.

Buy Put Options in Overbought Conditions:

- o When the RSI rises above a certain threshold (typically 70), it indicates overbought conditions, suggesting a potential selling opportunity. Consider buying Put options.

CONSIDERATIONS:

1. **Confirmation with Price Patterns:**

   - o Confirm RSI signals with price patterns or other technical indicators for added reliability.

2. **Dynamic Adjustments:**

   - Adjust the overbought and oversold thresholds based on the asset's historical behavior and current market conditions.

3. **Risk Management:**

   - Implement risk management practices, including setting stop-loss orders, to control potential losses.

EXECUTION STEPS:

1. **Plot RSI Indicator:**

   - Plot the RSI indicator on the price chart.

2. **Identify Overbought and Oversold Levels:**

   - Identify overbought conditions when the RSI rises above the overbought threshold (e.g., 70).

   - Identify oversold conditions when the RSI falls below the oversold threshold (e.g., 30).

3. **Execute Options Trade:**

   - Execute a Call option trade in oversold conditions.

   - Execute a Put option trade in overbought conditions.

4. **Monitor and Adjust:**

- o   Monitor the trade and be prepared to adjust or exit based on changing market conditions.

The RSI Overbought/Oversold Strategy is a popular approach for identifying potential reversal points based on the momentum of an asset. Traders should use this strategy in conjunction with other analysis tools and adapt it to their risk tolerance and trading style.

MOVING AVERAGE CROSSOVER STRATEGY

The Moving Average Crossover Strategy is a trend-following strategy that uses the crossover of two moving averages to identify potential entry and exit points in the market.

EXECUTION:

Buy Call Options on Bullish Crossover:

- o Look for a bullish crossover, where a short-term moving average crosses above a long-term moving average.

- o Consider buying Call options when this crossover occurs.

Buy Put Options on Bearish Crossover:

- o Look for a bearish crossover, where a short-term moving average crosses below a long-term moving average.

- o Consider buying Put options when this crossover occurs.

CONSIDERATIONS:

1. **Confirmation with Other Indicators:**

- Confirm crossover signals with other technical indicators or chart patterns for added reliability.

2. **Time Frame Adjustments:**

- Adjust the time frames of the moving averages based on the desired trading horizon. Shorter time frames may be suitable for day trading, while longer time frames may be suitable for swing trading.

3. **Dynamic Moving Average Types:**

- Experiment with different types of moving averages (e.g., simple moving average, exponential moving average) to find the most suitable for the asset being traded.

4. **Risk Management:**

- Implement risk management practices, including setting stop-loss orders, to control potential losses.

EXECUTION STEPS:

1. **Plot Moving Averages:**

- Plot two moving averages on the price chart, one short-term (e.g., 20-day) and one long-term (e.g., 50-day).

2. **Identify Crossovers:**

- o Look for crossovers between the short-term and long-term moving averages.

3. **Confirm Market Conditions:**

   - o Confirm the overall market conditions and trend direction.

4. **Execute Options Trade:**

   - o Execute a Call option trade on a bullish crossover.

   - o Execute a Put option trade on a bearish crossover.

5. **Monitor and Adjust:**

   - o Monitor the trade and be prepared to adjust or exit based on changing market conditions.

The Moving Average Crossover Strategy is a straightforward yet effective method for identifying potential trend reversals and entry points in the market. Traders should use this strategy in conjunction with other analysis tools and adapt it to their risk tolerance and trading style.

BOLLINGER BANDS VOLATILITY STRATEGY

The Bollinger Bands Volatility Strategy involves using Bollinger Bands to identify periods of high and low volatility in an asset's price, helping traders make informed decisions on potential entry and exit points.

EXECUTION:

- **Buy Call Options in Low Volatility:**

When the Bollinger Bands contract, indicating low volatility, consider buying Call options in anticipation of a potential price breakout.

- **Buy Put Options in High Volatility:**

When the Bollinger Bands expand, indicating high volatility, consider buying Put options in anticipation of a potential price reversal.

CONSIDERATIONS:

1. **Confirmation with Other Indicators:**

Confirm Bollinger Bands signals with other technical indicators or chart patterns for added reliability.

2. **Risk Management:**

Implement risk management practices, including setting stop-loss orders, to control potential losses.

3. **Adjusting Bollinger Bands Parameters:**

Experiment with adjusting the parameters of the Bollinger Bands (e.g., changing the standard deviation) based on the asset's characteristics and market conditions.

EXECUTION STEPS:

1. **Plot Bollinger Bands:**

Plot Bollinger Bands on the price chart, consisting of an upper band, a lower band, and a middle (20-day moving average) band.

2. **Identify Volatility Conditions:**

Observe the width of the Bollinger Bands. Narrow bands suggest low volatility, while widening bands suggest high volatility.

3. **Confirm Market Conditions:**

Confirm the overall market conditions and trend direction.

4. **Execute Options Trade:**

    o   Execute a Call option trade in low volatility conditions.

    o   Execute a Put option trade in high volatility conditions.

MONITOR AND ADJUST:

Monitor the trade and be prepared to adjust or exit based on changing market conditions.

The Bollinger Bands Volatility Strategy provides a dynamic approach to identifying potential market movements based on volatility levels. Traders should use this strategy in conjunction with other analysis tools and adapt it to their risk tolerance and trading style.

A SUPER TREND OPTION BUYING STRATEGY

A Super Trend option buying strategy involves incorporating the Super Trend indicator into the decision-making process for buying options. The Super Trend indicator helps identify the prevailing trend, and traders utilize this information to align their option buying strategies with the market direction.

COMPONENTS:

- **Trend Direction:**

The Super Trend determines whether the prevailing trend is bullish (uptrend) or bearish (downtrend).

- **Signal Line:**

A line is plotted above or below the price, indicating the direction of the trend.

IDENTIFYING TREND DIRECTION:

Traders use the Super Trend to identify the prevailing trend. This can be crucial for determining the type of options (call or put) to buy.

OPTION BUYING IN UPTREND:

- **Buy Call Options:**

In an uptrend (Super Trend indicating bullish), traders consider buying call options. Call options benefit from upward price movements.

OPTION BUYING IN DOWNTREND:

- **Buy Put Options:**

In a downtrend (Super Trend indicating bearish), traders may opt for buying put options. Put options profit from downward price movements.

RISK MANAGEMENT WITH SUPER TREND

Using Super Trend as a Stop-Loss:

Traders can set stop-loss levels based on the Super Trend line. Exiting a position if the price crosses the Super Trend line can help mitigate losses.

Adjusting Option Strategies:

If the Super Trend changes direction, traders may consider adjusting their option buying strategies accordingly. For example, shifting from buying call options in an uptrend to buying put options in a downtrend.

CONFIRMATION WITH OTHER INDICATORS

Relative Strength Index (RSI):

Confirming Super Trend signals with RSI can provide additional insights into the strength of a trend.

Volume Analysis:

Analyzing trading volumes alongside Super Trend signals can offer confirmation of the trend's sustainability.

CASE STUDY: APPLYING SUPER TREND TO OPTION BUYING

Example Scenario:

- The Super Trend indicator identifies an uptrend in a stock.

- Traders decide to buy call options with a strike price reflecting the expected upward movement.

- They set a stop-loss level based on the Super Trend line.

OUTCOME ANALYSIS:

- If the stock continues the uptrend, call options may yield profits.

- If the trend reverses, the stop-loss based on the Super Trend helps limit potential losses.

MEAN REVERSION OPTION BUYING

Introduction

Mean reversion is a financial theory suggesting that asset prices tend to revert to their historical average or mean over time. In options trading, a mean reversion option buying strategy involves identifying situations where the price of the underlying asset is expected to revert to its historical average, and traders capitalize on potential price movements by buying options.

Understanding Mean Reversion

Mean Reversion Theory: Mean reversion posits that if the price of an asset deviates significantly from its historical average, there is a tendency for it to move back toward that average over time.

Mean Reversion Option Buying Strategy

Identifying Mean Reversion Opportunities: Traders look for instances where the underlying asset's price has deviated significantly from its historical average, indicating a potential mean reversion opportunity.

Buying Options in Mean Reversion:

- *Buy Call Options:* When the asset's price is below its historical average and is expected to revert upward, traders may consider buying call options.

- *Buy Put Options:* Conversely, if the asset's price is above its historical average and is expected to revert downward, traders may opt for buying put options.

Risk Management in Mean Reversion Option Buying

Setting Stop-Loss Levels: Traders establish stop-loss levels to limit potential losses if the mean reversion doesn't occur as anticipated.

Time Decay Consideration: Since mean reversion strategies rely on the price returning to an average over time, traders should be mindful of the impact of time decay on option premiums.

Confirmation Indicators

Oscillators (e.g., RSI): Confirming mean reversion signals with oscillators, such as the Relative Strength Index (RSI), can provide additional insights into the potential strength of a reversal.

Moving Averages: Analyzing moving averages, especially shorter-term vs. longer-term averages, can help confirm mean reversion signals.

Case Study: Applying Mean Reversion to Option Buying

Example Scenario

1. **Stock XYZ:**

- Current Price: $80

- Historical Average: $100

2. **Mean Reversion Observation**: Traders notice a sharp decline in Stock XYZ from its historical average, indicating a potential mean reversion opportunity.

3. **Option Buying Strategy**: Traders buy call options with a strike price of $85, expecting an upward mean reversion.

4. **Risk Management**: A stop-loss is set at $75 to limit potential losses.

5. **Confirmation Indicators**:

   - RSI indicates oversold conditions.

   - Short-term moving averages are significantly below the long-term moving average.

6. **Outcome Analysis**:

   - If the mean reversion occurs, call options may yield profits.

   - If the deviation persists, the stop-loss helps limit potential losses.

7. **Adjustment Strategy:** Traders might consider adjustments based on new market information.

Conclusion

Mean reversion option buying strategies offer traders opportunities to capitalize on price movements expected to revert to historical averages. Successful implementation requires a thorough understanding of mean reversion principles, effective risk management, and confirmation from other indicators. Traders should continuously monitor market conditions and be prepared to adapt their strategies based on evolving trends. As with any trading approach, it is advisable to practice in simulated environments before deploying such strategies in live markets.

ICHIMOKU CLOUD

Using the Ichimoku Cloud in combination with option buying strategies can provide traders with a comprehensive approach to identifying potential entry and exit points, confirming trends, and managing risk. Here's how you might incorporate the Ichimoku Cloud into your option buying strategy:

TREND CONFIRMATION:

1. Uptrend Confirmation:

When the price is above the Cloud, it indicates an uptrend. Look for call option buying opportunities when the asset is in a clear uptrend.

2. Downtrend Confirmation:

When the price is below the Cloud, it suggests a downtrend. Consider put option buying opportunities when the asset is in a clear downtrend.

Crossover Signals:

3. Bullish Crossover:

Look for bullish option buying opportunities when the Tenkan Sen crosses above the Kijun Sen. This crossover suggests potential upward momentum.

4. Bearish Crossover:

Consider bearish option buying opportunities when the Tenkan Sen crosses below the Kijun Sen. This crossover signals potential downward momentum.

CLOUD BREAKOUT:

Bullish Cloud Breakout:

If the price moves above the Cloud, it may signal a potential bullish trend continuation. Consider call options.

Bearish Cloud Breakout:

If the price moves below the Cloud, it may indicate a potential bearish trend continuation. Consider put options.

Bullish Twist:

When Senkou Span A crosses above Senkou Span B, it forms a bullish twist. Consider call options as this suggests a potential bullish reversal.

Bearish Twist:

When Senkou Span A crosses below Senkou Span B, it forms a bearish twist. Consider put options as this suggests a potential bearish reversal.

Chikou Span and Past Prices:

Confirm trend strength by observing the position of Chikou Span concerning past prices. A Chikou Span above past prices in an uptrend or below past prices in a downtrend can strengthen the case for option buying.

RISK MANAGEMENT:

Setting Stop-Loss:

Establish tight stop-loss levels based on key support and resistance levels identified by the Cloud. This helps manage potential losses.

EXAMPLE SCENARIO:

Suppose you are considering option buying on a stock. You observe the following Ichimoku Cloud signals:

- Price is above the Cloud, indicating an uptrend.

- Bullish crossover with Tenkan Sen crossing above Kijun Sen.

- Bullish twist with Senkou Span A crossing above Senkou Span B.

These signals align, suggesting a strong potential uptrend. You might consider buying call options, setting a tight stop-loss below key support levels identified by the Cloud.

DO I OFFER A TRADING COURSE?

I do not offer courses through Google Meet or pre-recorded videos. If you're new to trading, particularly options trading, I offer guidance in live market environments. You're welcome to join me for a two-week trading class at my location, where I'll provide hands-on instruction and information regarding the high probability trading strategies that I use for my live trading, I will also teach you how to translate your trading strategies into algorithms for automated trading.

I limit each batch to a maximum of 10 people to ensure individual attention. Here are the details of the course:

1. Duration: 2 weeks
2. Classes commence on Sundays, covering market analysis and strategy selection based on prevailing conditions, including exclusive personal strategies not covered in standard resources.
3. Participants are required to have a minimum trading account balance of ₹50,000.
4. Instruction provided in both Malayalam and English.

5. Maximum of 10 participants per batch.
6. Free accommodation will be made available

Feel free to reach out for further information or to reserve your spot in the upcoming batch.

Fee-Very much affordable (Algo trading course is free)

You can contact me on
20masterstrategies@gmailcom
89219 78807 -WhatsApp

If this book has helped you understand the nuances of trading, even in the slightest way, **please consider leaving a review online, wherever you purchased it.** Your feedback matters. It helps other traders decide if this book could benefit them as well, and it helps me understand what resonated with readers so I can continue to produce valuable resources in the future.

Remember, we are all in this together. The trading community thrives on the shared exchange of ideas and the spirit of continuous improvement

www.ingramcontent.com/pod-product-compliance
Lightning Source LLC
Chambersburg PA
CBHW031139130726
47988CB00006B/2445